THE CAPTAIN'S LADY

THE CAPTAIN'S LADY
Ronald Morris

CHATTO & WINDUS

THE HOGARTH PRESS
LONDON

Published in 1985 by
Chatto & Windus. The Hogarth Press
40 William IV Street
London WC2N 4DF

British Library Cataloguing in Publication Data
Morris, Ronald
The captain's lady.
1. Fry, Beatie   2. Merchant seamen——
Training of——Great Britain——Biography
I. Title
387.5'092'4   HE569.F7

ISBN 0–7011–2946–8

Phototypeset by Wyvern Typesetting Limited, Bristol

Printed in Great Britain by
Redwood Burn Ltd
Trowbridge, Wiltshire

To Jean and Louise Diana

'And let me speak to th' yet unknowing world
How these things came about . . .'

Contents

Illustrations

Preface

A woman stands a few feet from a ship's gun with a boy of thirteen bound hand and foot over the breech. He is being flogged by a man in nautical uniform. Lined up nearby are 150 boys of similar age, rigid with fear, there to 'witness punishment'. The entire proceedings, even to the number of lashes of the cane meted out, take place at the woman's behest.

Unlikely as it may seem, this scene took place in this century. It occurred hundreds of times in the course of the thirty-eight years that Beatrice Holme Fry was virtually commander of the Training Ship *Mercury*, a nautical school for boys on the banks of the Hamble River in Southern England.

In 1945, as a boy of fifteen with no clear idea of what I wanted to do in life, I decided to go to sea in the Merchant Navy. Since I could start only when I was sixteen I was sent to the *Mercury* where I encountered Mrs Fry in the last seven months of her life. The impression she made was such that I determined, even at that early age, to discover the circumstances that led to her being the effective director of an all-male establishment. It was a role she had sustained, seemingly without effort, since 1908. In my research I was to discover that she had prepared for her role for twenty-three years before that. It goes without saying that there can be few instances – if any – of a woman at that time proving so successful in an adjunct to what was probably regarded as the most manly of occupations, seafaring – and this at a time when the rules of society, and especially of the class into which she was born, debarred most women from roles that were other than menial, domestic or decorative. She may prove to have been the last great unsung character of her generation.

R M

I – *The Mercury*

Behind a remarkable man it is just possible there might be a more remarkable woman. This was certainly the case with C. B. Fry, who died in 1956 at eighty-four years of age. He was described by one of his obituarists as a giant of this century, and by John Arlott as 'perhaps the most variously gifted Englishman of any age'.[1] For J. B. Priestley a list of men who were most characteristically English had to include Fry, together with Raleigh, Pepys, Samuel Johnson, Charles Lamb, Michael Faraday, and Richard Burton the explorer; and he wrote of him that 'I have a special fondness for versatile men, natural all-rounders, arising belatedly among us from the Renaissance, men who even in their own time loomed as legendary figures.'[2]

Priestley never met Fry, but his judgement was unerring insofar as his admiration was for the man as a natural all-rounder. The variety of his accomplishments in sport – he had only to take up a game to master it – leaves intact his title as the greatest sportsman that ever lived. Yet although Fry was a brilliant scholar and writer, the friend and confidant of world figures, some of whom turned to him for counsel, his wife, Beatrice Holme Fry, dwarfed him in spite of all his gifts. In a more generous time, and given the freedom and also the education that women of her class were denied, or may even have despised, she could have led nations. What made her even more remarkable is that she fought hard at concealment, at exercising her powers in a limited area with huge success, while successfully keeping the world outside her gates unaware of them.

C. B. Fry, or simply C.B. – such was his fame that the initials were known to everybody, and everybody knew there was only one C.B. –

was to be found in 1945 presiding as Captain Superintendent of the Training Ship *Mercury*, a nautical school for boys based on the Hamble River six miles from Southampton. He had been there for thirty-seven years, his huge talents dissipated, so many believed, in an enterprise that might have provided congenial employment for a retired sea captain and half a dozen ex-Royal Navy petty officers. What was worse, in the eyes of the limited circle which knew of his situation, was that his captaincy was only nominal. His wife ran the school, and did so with harsh efficiency.

The parents of a boy wishing to join the ship in 1945 would be sent a prospectus in which Mrs Fry appeared as joint director of the ship with her husband. He would not know until he got to the *Mercury* that he was about to encounter one of the most dynamic women of her generation and the true commander of that establishment.

The prospectus seemed to offer an exciting life in novel surroundings. A picture of the grounds depicted a signal mast of terrifying height, with smiling boys in smart uniform posed on the rigging that held it in place. On the river there was a ship of sorts, the sloop HMS *Gannet*, renamed *President*, which had been built for the Navy in 1878. Stripped of her masts, rigging and funnel, she had been given an additional deck, and the whole had been roofed over with corrugated iron. To some it looked like a Noah's Ark or a huge houseboat anchored in the middle of the river, to others, familiar with life on board, she was a descendant of the prison hulks of the time of Dickens. With her six gunports open wide the main deck was massively exposed to the elements, and in winter the upper deck was as cold inside as it was out. Only those who have experienced the English climate with the minimum of protection can appreciate how brutally inhospitable it is for at least six months of the year, and on the ship the *Mercury* boys experienced it at first hand, being spared only the fall of rain and snow directly onto their canvas hammocks.

If there was a warning of hardships to come it was not to be found in the prospectus, but in a peculiar document directed to the parents of boys headed for the *Mercury*. It began 'Life is a fight from birth to Home'. It was an arresting thought that its author appeared to regard death as Home – adding extra emphasis with a capital letter, which mere birth did not warrant. The document went on:

Periods come in everyone's life when it is struggle or slip back, fight or go under; these periods are not incessant in a landman's life; there is an easing up, a breathing space afforded them when they can survey their position with a certain amount of complacency and safety. Those who take the sea for a career know little of this lull; they admire the sea, they respect the sea, they like the sea, they love the sea, but they have to fight her twenty-four hours of the day. This life-long fight needs sturdy frames and valiant hearts. Bodies fit enough to bear extremes of heat and cold; hearts brave enough to take hard knocks and yet stand up again to fight and win.

TS *Mercury* is not a school; it is not a training school – the *Mercury* is a ship. As a ship she has an atmosphere, a life and a body with a just and kindly heart. The routine is hard; tasks are arduous and discipline strict. Only boys with the sea in their blood can take the life and flourish. The *Mercury* tradition is high. Each boy has it in his own care.

Should your boy be strong enough in body and staunch enough in heart, TS *Mercury* can send him forth to the Seven Seas – very sure of his ability to fight and win.

> '. . . and by the vision splendid
> Is on his way attended.'[3]

Students of literary style could tell at once that it was not the work of C.B., while the content could hardly be the work of one who, apart from the common enough hardships of prep and public school, had probably not known a day's real hardship in his life, and whose experience of ships and the sea was nil – if one left aside the occasional foray abroad travelling first-class on an ocean liner. An old sailor might have said that it had been written by someone whose last ship was a square rigger – and that so long ago that time had dulled the memory and erased the record of months of monumental boredom that occurred even on sailing ships, months which were sporadically offset by spells of frantic activity in heavy weather. Nor

13

did the author realise that boredom was an even greater problem on power-driven ships. Possibly it might have been written by a romantic soul with a hankering for the books of 'Taffrail' and Marryat, or a weakness for the poems of John Masefield. But if it was dishonest or naive about life at sea, it was at least direct in telling parents that life for their sons on the *Mercury* was going to be hell; and if there were any doubts in the mind of the new boys about who was in charge of the *Mercury* they were dispelled on his first weekend, for on Saturday Mrs Fry inspected the ship's company, an experience that would leave its members marked for life.

By comparison the appearance of C.B. on Sunday morning for the same purpose was a tame affair. The boys, 148 of them aged between twelve to sixteen, assembled in two long lines facing each other across a strip of asphalt which ran down one side of the twenty-five-room mansion in which C.B. and his wife lived and which was known to everybody as the 'House'. C.B. appeared before them at about ten o'clock in his uniform of Hon. Captain R N R. Occasionally he would wear his greatcoat with the collar turned up, arousing the suspicion that it concealed the informal garb of somebody taken against his will from a quiet Sunday morning with the papers.

At seventy-three C. B. Fry was the epitome of dignified old age – erect, clear-eyed and relaxed. The word 'patrician' was often employed by those who tried to describe a man who had spent half a century in the public eye. If hackneyed, it was appropriate. There was in the aristocratic profile the restrained hauteur of one who wanted to appear confident in noble lineage, with every assurance that his account of himself, could modesty be waived, would reveal one who was a gentleman, but above all an English gentleman with the best credentials, a public school education, years at university, and a distinguished career. His air was essentially that of the *amateur* whose skills were concealed and who would only exercise them publicly with reluctance, but then with an *élan* which would dismay the professional. Such a figure should perhaps have excited awe, perhaps even fear and a blind devotion. He was accorded instead the benign admiration given to a retired sportsman.

C.B. would screw his monocle into his right eye and amiably submit to being steered along the lines by one of his staff, as if he were a distinguished visitor alighting from an aeroplane and obliged to inspect a Guard of Honour before leaving for lunch at the Palace. It was perfunctory, but it was pleasurable when contrasted with what had taken place the previous day.

On Saturday the boys would assemble in the same place to be inspected by Mrs Fry. They brought with them their entire meagre kit, each one making a neat pile on the ground of spare uniform, marching and football boots, oilskins, overalls and toothbrush. Incongruously there rested on top of the pile his dirty pyjamas, brought ashore from the dormitory ship that morning, and his handkerchief, which he had had for a week and was damp, as a result of his having scrubbed it on the floor of the showers earlier that morning. There had been three hours of frantic preparation to get all this ready, with brief interruptions to go to the showers, breakfast and chapel. Fear contended with hunger as the dominant element in the lives of these boys, but never was fear more apparent than on this morning when they would come face to face with the terrifying Mrs Fry.

Less frightened, perhaps, but suitably in awe of the lady was the staff of instructors. They too would be on parade at the moment she appeared, some of them grouped in front of a small clock tower at one end of the asphalt strip, the others between the lines of boys. Those between the lines were called Watch Officers, the equivalent of house-masters in other schools.

The staff consisted of seven or eight men who were referred to as officers, though none of them had held officer status in either the armed forces or the Merchant Navy. For the most part they were ex-petty officers of the Royal Navy, the hard men of the lower deck who looked faintly incongruous in uniforms with one or two gold stripes apiece in near-imitation of those worn by Naval Officers. More at ease in their uniforms, and infinitely more skilled in their subject, were the band masters, a trio of men whose professionalism and numbers – three to teach music where only one taught seamanship – showed the weight attached to music in the curriculum. The senior man wore three stripes. He was a short, broad-shouldered man of craggy good looks with a pleasant husky voice and, whether or not he had seen the inside of an officers' mess, an unmistakable air of command. Harold Fraser was styled the Chief Officer, and had been on the staff for over twenty years.

At ten o'clock Fraser looked about him for the last time before going into the House to fetch Mrs Fry, leaving the company standing at ease, waiting. When he returned he was still alone. He came out of the door, went to a point in the middle of the asphalt and turned round. A minute of so later, slowly but steadily, walking stick in hand, the ruler of this gathering emerged. The Chief Officer called everybody to attention and raised his right hand to his cap in salute. His colleagues did the same. The look on his face never varied. It was that mixture of awe, fear and blind devotion which her husband so signally failed to inspire.

Mrs Fry's first act was to nod to the men near the clock tower and wish them 'Good morning' in a deep gruff voice. The men saluted again and departed, leaving behind the Watch Officers and Mr Fraser.

Mrs Fry wore a uniform of sorts. Her navy-blue double-breasted jacket was modelled on those of her officers, with eight buttons. It had the two larger pockets of the male jacket but no breast pocket. Above where the pocket should have been she wore the ribbon of the OBE. Just visible below an ankle-length skirt were thick woollen stockings and brightly polished black shoes, each topped with a silver buckle. There were superstitions attached to the colour of the stockings; red if she was in a bad mood, yellow if her mood was good. More often than not she wore red. Her hat was round with a high crown and a wide brim, and the thick band of material round the crown carried a brass badge. Under her jacket she wore a white shirt and a black tie, and thick leather gloves completed the costume. Judging by the antiquated style and faded material, it was the very same uniform that she had worn in 1927, when the then Prince of Wales had visited the ship, and again in 1929 when his brother HRH the Duke of York, later King George VI, had spent the day there.

She was now eighty-three. Her ancient face was deeply lined and she had a thin bloodless mouth of jolting severity. Pale little moles on her cheeks sprouted grey hairs, and she had the tiny moustache of the very elderly woman who has ceased to care about appearances. She was of average height, but men who remembered her in younger days described her as a big woman whose progress through the day was that of a great ship under full sail, a sort of Volumnia, so formidable was her presence. In spite of her years she squared her shoulders like the boys she was about to inspect, and held her head in a faintly arrogant tilt.

'Where shall we begin, Mr Fraser?'

This was said in a measured way, the words spaced out as if they were some sort of currency, and hard currency at that, to be dispensed grudgingly and to the maximum possible effect. She could produce fear in a boy, and probably in a man too, with a long steady look, followed by two words of censure that left him quaking.

Fraser took her to the first boy in one of the long rows and began the business of picking over the piles of kit set neatly on the ground. For up to two hours she moved steadily up and down the lines looking intently at hundreds of garments. Her short sight meant that they generally had to be waved under her nose. The Chief Officer hovered at her shoulder, notebook in hand, obviously deeply anxious that everything should be to her satisfaction. If things were not so, he scribbled numbers and details on a page and looked at the offender in a meaningful way. A resistant stain, a button loose, a boot inadequately laced, counted as capital crimes. With naval precision, each item was picked up to an exact rhythm and similarly replaced.

There were curious rituals which were unknown outside the *Mercury* – certainly not in Divisions, the inspection carried out in naval establishments of which this exercise was supposed to be an equivalent. The boys had, for example, to bend down in unison and pull up their trouser legs for Mrs Fry to inspect their bootlaces. Then another order was shouted in that curiously strangled voice peculiar to parade grounds, the last word exploding into the air like a hand grenade going off:

'Pick up toothbrushes and *handkerchiefs*!'

They went down again and came upright holding the named items, damp hankie in the left hand, toothbrush in the right. On the order 'Show teeth!' they held out the left hand in a mad parody of a Nazi salute and brought the right up so that the toothbrush reposed, bristles outwards, against the bottom lip. At the same time they bared their front teeth in a hideous grin, and once again the slow progress took place and each boy was minutely examined.

There followed a moment of chilling embarrassment for Fraser when he had to order the boys to pick up their pyjama bottoms and hold them out at arm's length. Mrs Fry trudged along the lines, peering intently at each soiled garment. No one had any illusions about what she was looking for, but she need not have bothered. Life for the boys was so tough and so exhausting that sex never reared its head, and dirty pyjama bottoms yielded no evidence of what the Scout Movement used to describe as 'beastliness'. What the boys did not know was that the lady in search of tell-tale stains, who would punish mercilessly if she found them, had been one whose own passions had triggered off the chain of events that placed her before them on that Saturday morning.

When it was all over, and the grim, mirthless, ancient lady had returned to the House, there was a universal feeling of relief, almost of euphoria. The boys cleared everything away and went lightheartedly on to the next piece of routine, a gruelling hour of drill on the playing field with old Lee Enfield rifles and bayonets.

There were other aspects of life on the ship, if such were needed, that stamped indelibly on the minds of all present the power over their lives of the woman in charge. The boys went barefoot winter and summer, wearing boots only for parades and inspections and on dry evenings when they marched to the pier on their way to the dormitory ship; on wet evenings they tied their boots together by the laces and hung them round their necks. Gloves and scarves were not part of the uniform, and hats spent most of their time in store. The only warmth to be had came from vigorous activity, and a dreaded punishment was to be made to stand motionless on a cold day next to a flagstaff near the House. No one told them that these hardships had been instituted by Mrs Fry sixty years earlier, when she was a vigorous young woman in her early twenties, and that she had endured them herself, along with those on whom she had inflicted them.

To the discomforts of bare feet and the general hardships of everyday life at the *Mercury* were added restrictions that made it seem like a prison for those inside – one with an open gate, perhaps, but almost impossible to escape from. Repeatedly during the day the order was given to 'Muster All Hands', to count heads and account for everybody not present. If a boy decided to run away he would have little more than half an hour's start before he was missed, and an hour at the most.

At nine o'clock every evening the boys prepared to go to the dormitory ship. A group went ahead of the main body, going out by dinghy to fetch two cutters from their moorings on the river and bring them to the pier for the rest to get into. Life-jackets were never worn; there wasn't one in the place, and if a boat had gone down the loss of life would have been appalling. Booted and wearing heavy oilskins over the denim overalls they were going to need at 'Clean Ship' the following morning, they would never have stood a chance if a grossly over-laden cutter had succumbed to the ferocity of a winter's gale bellowing up the Hamble. Yet they took the risk without a thought, made nonchalant by repetition and the simple necessity of having to get to where they could sleep. Life had indeed been lost over the years. Tied up to the ship was a seldom-used cutter called the *Maurice Driver* after a boy who had gallantly but fruitlessly dived into the river one black night to bring back a shipmate who had fallen overboard.

They piled into the boats, so many of them packed so tightly in the stern-sheets, under the thwarts and in the bows, that the gunwales – the upper sides of the boats – were barely clear of the water. Only in the most violent storms was thought given to the possibility that this might be dangerous, and more journeys made by a cutter with fewer people on board, and with a specially picked rough-weather crew on the oars.

The shipboard routine could be simple and quick. On the main deck, in spaces between the guns, the boys assembled in four groups, thirty-seven to a group, two to starboard and two to port, facing inboard. Within each group were three sections of twelve, with their Section Leaders at their head. The whole was called a Watch, and had a Leading Hand in charge.

The first job was to get the hammocks slung. Half of the company, consisting mainly of the older boys, went to the upper deck, and the rest to the orlop deck, much of which was below the waterline and thus marginally the warmer of the two in winter.

The hammocks slung, the boys returned to the main deck, undressed and got into pyjamas. At this moment they could never quite be sure that the logical next step would take place, whereby the roll would be called and, after some unusual bits of ritual, they would all be dismissed to their hammocks. Once in a while, the duty officer was moved to assert himself in a way that reminded everybody that he was very much in command; and since on still nights the sounds of activity on the ship, including much shouting of orders and loud bugle calls, carried to the House, the people there would get the message too. As long as he did not hit anyone he could be as peremptory as he liked.

On this particular night Mr Stark is on duty. The boys are assembled on the main deck, shivering in the cold air blasting through the open gunports. Mr Stark stands amidships, the bugler close at hand, and looks about for an excuse to administer a 'shake-up', the term used to describe the flurry of excessive discipline demanded by Mrs Fry when she imagines the boys are getting slack. He announces that the exercise of slinging hammocks was too noisy and took far too long.

In the apprehensive silence that follows, he walks to the ship's bell at the fore end of the main deck and rings it briskly – the signal for Fire Stations. The boys explode into action, like milling ants. In seconds they have closed the gunports, covered various hatches, and done a score of jobs connected with the exercise. Mr Stark shouts, 'Bugler! Sound the "Still".' The four ascending notes have an electric effect. There is instant silence. Everybody freezes.

'Fire starboard side for'ard!' he shouts. 'Carry on!'

Two more notes on the bugle and pandemonium is resumed.

A hose is run out, one end is clamped to a rotary pump on the after deck and the other fitted with a nozzle and pointed through an opening in the ship's side near the mythical fire. More orders follow, each emphasised by a bugle call.

'Heave round!'

Four boys seize the pump handle and swing it round with gusto. The hose fills and little drops of water appear on its surface which hang momentarily and then slide off to form pools on the deck. The jet of water shoots from the nozzle, and soon a sound as of heavy rain drifts back to the ship as it falls on the surface of the darkened river.

' 'Vast heaving!'

The pump stops and the tired, angry, helpless company waits in suspense for the next order. At this late hour, when the 'Last Post' should long since have sounded and the rows of stretched hammocks received their exhausted burdens, will he go the whole hog?

He does.

'Abandon ship!'

There is a rush to the boats, and in seconds the ship's company, clad only in pyjamas, is afloat. Only the bugler and Mr Stark remain on board.

'Take your boats round the ship and return on board,' he shouts into the darkness.

Back on board it takes ten minutes to mop up the mess of the fire drill, hang up wet lengths of hose, re-open the gunports and get the routine back to the point at which it had been interrupted when Mr Stark rang the bell. Now follows a moment of ritual which must make him wince every time he comes to it. He is a middle-aged ex-petty officer, demobilised in the closing weeks of the Second World War, who has spent most of his working life in the Royal Navy. He has survived the boring years of peace and the three-year stints on foreign stations. He has survived the hell of the North Atlantic and the double hell of the Russian convoys, when German ships and aircraft had battered his ship, and when – according to legend – he had often picked up the bloody remains of a casualty, put them in a bucket and unceremoniously dumped them into the sea. Coarsened by his experiences, he must nevertheless set in train a quasi-religious ritual which is part of his job at the *Mercury*, the best job he has ever had for the excellent reason that it is on a ship that is going nowhere. If he appears to be losing his touch, it's the sack and back to real ships again and all the misery he has escaped. Mrs Fry knows that for every man she employs there are thousands queuing behind him for similar work where they can use their nautical skills without having to go to sea. For this reason her staff live in fear of her, and do exactly as she says.

'Port Watches, about turn!'

With this order Mr Stark brings the boys who had their backs to the pier facing in that direction along with those on the starboard side of the ship.

'Kneel!'

All go down on their knees. There is a flutter of hands as the few Roman Catholics in the ranks genuflect. For two minutes they stay there in utter silence, perhaps the first real silence there has been that day. Some kneel uncomplainingly on the damp patches made by the fire hose. By now all of them are past caring about the bone-chilling cold.

Mr Stark can be forgiven for pondering the meaning of this part of the evening ritual, wondering to what extent they are being asked to kneel and address themselves to their Maker, and how much of it is an obeisance to the people in the House (which everybody is obliged to face). Perhaps it crosses his mind that they are like adherents of a religious sect whose prayers will have no weight unless they are made in a prescribed direction, towards the birth-place of a prophet or the place where that prophet has taken off for the next world.

Mr Stark speaks again.

'Stand. Bugler, sound the note.'

A solitary note is given, and they sing:

> 'So be our rest Thy palaces most fair,
> Not built with hands, whose stones Thy praise declare,
> Where war is not, and all Thy sons are free,
> Where Thou art known, and all is known in Thee.'

Presumably Mr Stark is aware of the irony. They sing of celestial palaces, freedom and a knowingness beyond all human understanding, when he has subjected them in this austere barrack of a ship, to an attack on even that little freedom left to them, the freedom to escape in sleep from the hardships of the day, and all for reasons beyond their comprehension.

The singing carries across the water, across the reeds by the river bank, and up to an open window on the first floor of the house. In deep chairs by the window two women sit listening – Mrs Fry and a Miss Hoare who is in her early sixties, about whom the boys know nothing except that she bears the surname of the man who founded the *Mercury* in 1885.

They heard the commands, the bugle calls, and now they hear the singing. They heard, no doubt with satisfaction, the change in the routine which they had established. They hear the final bugle call of the day, 'Last Post', and then watch as the lights on the ship go out, one by one. At last they too prepare for sleep, satisfied that they are still in absolute command of the most remarkable school in England.

In another part of the House C.B. lies in bed, not asleep but staring at the ceiling, as he recites aloud a ball-by-ball account of a cricket match that took place half a century ago.

2 – *The Young Adventurers*

The year 1885 was not only that in which Charles Hoare founded
the *Mercury*. It was also the year in which he appeared in a London
court with a young woman to answer charges arising out of his long
association with her, beginning when the latter was barely into her
teens, when Charles was twice her age, married, and the father of
four children. The young woman was Beatrice Holme Sumner –
Beatie to her family, and later Mrs Fry. Their origins and his means
were such that their presence in the Court of Chancery and the
likelihood of a prison sentence seemed faintly incongruous. At risk
with them were several of Beatie's relatives, most notably her cousin,
Winifred Ida, Lady Cholmondeley, wife of the Marquess of
Cholmondeley, Joint Hereditary Great Chamberlain of England and
thus one of the figures closest to the monarch. It was an event which
ravaged the lives of people close to them, and left others socially
embarrassed.

Beatie was born on 12 July 1862 at Hatchlands, a well-appointed
mansion in Surrey a few miles east of Guildford. An ancestor,
William Brightwell Sumner, had purchased the house from Admiral
Boscawen in the previous century, and her father, Arthur Sumner,
had inherited it. The Sumners had been a heterogeneous family:
rich merchants, landowners, the odd academic. One had been
Provost of King's College, Cambridge. Beatie's Aunt Georgiana,
her father's sister, was married to Lord Fitzhardinge of Berkeley
Castle, and her mother's sister was a Kingscote from the eponymous
village in Gloucestershire. Beatie Sumner was descended from the
kings of Denmark and of England; the relatives of her childhood, in
whose houses she and her parents were welcome guests, included

the Duke of Beaufort, Lord Bathurst and Lord Bloomfield, and her cousins could be discovered in many of the great country houses of the British Isles.

Little is known about Beatie's early life, for much of the evidence was destroyed in a bonfire of her papers and pictures immediately after her death. Tales told at second and third hand by descendants of the Kingscote, Sumner and Hoare families suggest that from an early age she was remarkable for her strong will and defiant nature, and almost impossible to control. The conventions of Victorian society dictated that she should be given over to a nannie and a governess, who would combine to teach her manners and the limited range of skills and subjects deemed suitable preparation for a girl whose aim in life was marriage, the rearing of children and discreet idleness. In her unsettled childhood Beatie escaped these measures, and instead of learning to read she learned to ride, spending as much time as possible with horses. Her command of them mirrored the command she exercised at home, where servants, many of them mature men and women, were subordinate to their employer's children. From an early age Beatie had what might be best described as natural arrogance, a sense of power over others that surpassed mere belief or conviction.

By the time she was twelve she had the reputation of an adventurer, of being a distinctive personality with an insistent nature, vivacious, enthusiastic and impulsive. She was barely literate, but she had the capacity to learn, to apply herself with a terrifying single-mindedness to the ideas and activities she thought important.

While there seems to have been a conspiracy to destroy any revealing records, a book which survived the bonfire may shed some oblique light on the personality of the youthful Beatie. A biography by Mrs Alexander of Jane Welsh Carlyle, the wife of the well-known essayist, historian and philosopher, was published in 1891: Charles Hoare bought a copy the following year, and it bears his signature and Beatie's initials in her own hand.

There are no marks on the book apart from the signature and initials, no marginal notes or dashes to indicate that Charles saw the character of the woman he loved reflected in its pages, but it could be that the description of Jane as a child was a fair approximation to Beatie at the same age – fiery, strong-willed, aggressive, not above punching someone who got in the way, and utterly fearless.

Documentation of Beatie's life begins in her early teens, by which time she was disturbingly mature. Adult women were dismayed at the attention she drew from their menfolk. At about this time she achieved what C. B. Fry's biographer, Denzil Batchelor, described as 'an unusual double'.[1] She was made an honorary whip of the Duke of Beaufort's Hounds, and was the model for a painting by G. F. Watts which was meant as a tribute to her as a 'celebrated beauty' of her generation. She was, however, handsome rather than beautiful, with a high forehead which, in later years, she emphasised by wearing her hair very short. She had calm eyes that looked steadily at people, seeming to see more of their personalities than they would have liked to give away. Her mouth was firm with lips much fuller than one would expect in a woman who, in old age, was noted for her thin, aggressive mouth. Her straight nose and a chin that jutted slightly completed a face that was full of determination and strength of character.

The placid Gloucestershire countryside of the mid-1870s was stirred by her appearance in the hunting field; the great packs of the area – the Beaufort, the Vale of White Horse (known to everybody as the 'V.W.H.') and the Cotswold – had an unusually large turn-out of members who wanted to see her in action, as she rode with a courage and a skill far beyond her years.

Whilst little is known of Beatie the child, even less is known of her parents. Her mother was undoubtedly an inadequate and pathetic woman whose ill judgement in the matter of her daughter's conduct fuelled the disaster that was to envelop the whole family. Her father seemed pale and ineffectual, insufficiently forceful to stand up to his daughter. Both parents, it is said, were torn between pride in their daughter's riding accomplishments, and despair at their inability to control her. Their grip on Beatie's young life was further diminished when Mrs Sumner found that her daughter could be more decisive and shrewder than herself in domestic matters. One cannot discipline a child one moment and then consult her the next without some loss of authority.

Beatie was living with her parents in Cheltenham when her appearance and her extraordinary character began to draw attention. The family had arrived in the town in 1874, after spending the previous five years on the move. A down-turn in their fortunes had left them unable to maintain their home and the standard of living they preferred, so their property, Hatchlands, was rented out to other people, notably Count Haryett de Bechevet and his Hungarian wife Marianne.

The five itinerant years may well have proved traumatic to a girl reared in a stately home. From 1869, when Beatie was only seven, the lofty rooms and corridors of Hatchlands were exchanged for a series of houses in the towns and cities of Gloucestershire. Of necessity Beatie's parents had to adjust their standard of living to the rent they exacted from letting Hatchlands. Where there had been stability of place, with a predictable calendar of events, familiar social exchanges, and loyal servants constantly on hand, there were now uncertainties, the repeated need to re-assert themselves at each new address. In the highly stratified society of late nineteenth-century England they must have been all too aware of the gap between their way of life and that of noble relatives still secure in houses as good or better than Hatchlands. If nobility has its obligations, it also has its penalties. Beatie's father could not make money in ways unbecoming to a gentleman. Although he was an authority on farm animals, in demand as a judge at the county agricultural shows of the day, sharing the duties with men like the Duke of Beaufort and Charles Hoare, he could not descend to trading in the cattle markets and turn his expertise to account by buying and selling animals in competition with auctioneers, dealers and butchers. Yet he desperately needed the money. In Cheltenham he became Master of the Cotswold Hunt, a post that meant additional expenditure if he was to satisfy the expectations of the club members, and he did so against mounting debts. The uneducated Beatie had been acquiring an education of sorts, of the kind that would never have been granted her had she remained sheltered into her teens in the elegant surroundings of Hatchlands. She had been made tough and decisive, and could handle people in ways that went beyond merely being 'good with servants'.

Beatie Sumner met Charles Hoare – appropriately enough – on the hunting field, though stories surviving into this century would have us believe otherwise. Her good looks and precocity drew the attention of men to the extent that they forgot they were meeting someone who was still a child. It is said that Charles was invited to meet her at Berkeley Castle, where his hosts, Lord and Lady Fitzhardinge, would turn a blind eye while he made heavy overtures to Beatie, perhaps to the point of seducing her. This, it was hoped, would have the effect of frightening her off men – a necessary step, her relatives thought, since she was obviously enjoying the effect she had on the opposite sex. The plot failed, the story goes, when Beatie seduced her would-be seducer. As we will see, the story of any meeting between Charles and Beatie at Berkeley is so improbable that it is surprising that it has survived so long; but there may be a germ of truth in the belief that Beatie was the dominant partner in the relationship. She was barely fifteen when her father was first moved to upbraid Charles for his ardent pursuit of the girl: Beatie, significantly, did nothing to discourage her admirer.

Charles was born on 18 May 1847, at a house in Birdcage Walk, London, the son of Peter Richard Hoare, a partner in Hoare's Bank, Fleet Street, a banking business which is still extant and still run by the same family. His mother was Lady Sophia, daughter of Lord Romney, the second Earl. Her home was Kelsey Manor, Beckenham, on the outskirts of London, described by an estate agent when it came on the market at the end of the century as 'suitable for a nobleman or gentleman of fortune'.[2] Charles was to inherit this, and a great deal more besides, but his childhood was spent not at Kelsey but at Luscombe Castle in Devon, another of his father's properties and equally grand.

Luscombe Castle was Charles's home, and the school in which he was to be groomed for high office in the family business. He was no scholar. An account of his boyhood says that he had little taste for the classics, literature, and the gentler arts, 'the constraints of ordered boyhood being abhorrent to him. His school was the Devonshire fields, his university the world.'[3] Others describe his childhood in less charitable terms, with touches that suggest a startling resemblance to Beatie's early life. He was an impossible child – self-willed, riding rough-shod over all attempts to have him conform. Although most of his family went to public schools he was spared this, probably because he was slightly lame or, as Beatie later described it, 'he walked a little late'.

Oddly enough, his lameness was at the root of his brilliance as a sportsman. He drove himself to excel in cricket, playing on equal terms with county players. Cricket was a lifelong passion, and one which was to bring him into contact with C. B. Fry: the young C.B., playing near his Chislehurst home in Kent in the 1890s, inevitably met the ageing Charles, who freely spent his money to entertain those who were talented at the sport he loved. Charles also excelled at tennis, but above all at horsemanship. Astride a horse his disability vanished; he looked and felt supremely confident, and in time came to be acknowledged as one of the finest riders in the country. He grew into a big amiable bear of a man, over six feet tall, with no taste for banking, but a vast appetite for the good things in life – by which he meant property, horses and yachts, which his stake in the bank and his subsequent inheritance could pay for. The yachts were not mere playthings, however. One was moored at Exmouth and was used to train local boys, who then found jobs in other private yachts. A few went into the Royal Navy.

When Charles and Beatie met they must have felt the rapport of people whose experiences, personalities, drives and skills were in many respects identical. Like was attracted to like, it appeared, with irresistible urgency. There were, however, certain obstacles to the liaison. For a start in 1867 Charles had married Margaret Baring Short, of Bickham House in Devon. Curiously enough, though Luscombe Castle and Bickham were not many miles apart, his letter asking for an interview with Mr Baring Short to discuss marriage with Margaret was addressed from a nearby hotel, and for the rest of his life Luscombe barely featured in his travels. On the surface the two young people were well matched. Both came from 'good' families, with a sprinkling of noble relatives and ancestors on both sides; both were well off, and moved among their peers with all the self-assurance of the Victorian upper classes. The differences between them, however, were considerable. Charles was a man for the outdoors, happy to spend every day of the long hunting season in the saddle, and turning to his yachts, to cricket and to tennis in the summer. When he went to London it was to enjoy club life at Boodle's rather than the theatre and concerts, and there is little to suggest that he read anything other than the papers and journals.

Margaret, by contrast, was a petite, pretty woman, more cerebral in her pleasures. A portrait of her as a young woman suggests a shy person, with a wide forehead and gentle eyes. Her boldest features were her dark hair and black arching eyebrows. Her first love was music. She had a rich contralto voice and appeared in concerts which she organised with her friends to raise money for charities. Mozart was her favourite composer, judging from the programmes. If Margaret and Charles had any taste in common it lay in their appreciation of furniture, paintings and antiques, with Charles eventually specialising in nautical artefacts such as models of the great men-o'-war of previous centuries.

They had four sons and a daughter, but one son died after an accident in which he broke his neck.

It was soon after their marriage that Charles came into the public eye, as becomes apparent from Margaret's scrapbook of cuttings, which spanned thirty years of their lives and ran to over a thousand items. Unfortunately most of the items are undated, nor is it clear what newspapers and journals they are from, but the collection is remarkable for its candour. One of the earliest cuttings tells of her husband's unfortunate experiences with a 'notorious speculator' on the Stock Exchange, and this is bracketed with another, undated like the first, with no indication of the paper in which it appeared. It is worth quoting in full:

One of the current topics of 'Town' gossip is the tremendous failure of the younger member of a well known banking firm who has 'gone' for the enormous sum of £400,000 on the Stock Exchange. The young man was some little time ago a rather warm patron of the Turf, and showed some disposition to 'plunge' in a mild sort of way. The senior partners feared that if it came to the ears of the public that one of the firm was in any way connected with the Turf it might affect their credit for respectability, so at their request the young man abandoned the Turf and took to gambling on the Stock Exchange, with the happy result I have named.[4]

The current equivalent of £400,000 lost in the 1860s would be in the region of £9 million.

Most of the earliest cuttings, however, deal with the revival of coaching and of her husband's part in it. After the rapid spread of railways there grew up a nostalgia for the days of coaches with teams of horses and all the colourful paraphernalia that went with them. The prime mover in this was the Duke of Beaufort, who started a joint stock company in the summer of 1866 with shares of £10 each. Significantly for Charles's fortunes, most of the shareholders came from Gloucestershire. A coach called Old Times was put on the old mail road through Croydon, Reigate and Hickstead, with the London terminus in Piccadilly and the Brighton one in Castle

Square. Charles put his coach, Exquisite, on the road in 1867 and ran it all winter on a scheduled service between Beckenham and Sevenoaks. The coach owners did not merely finance them – they drove them as well, vying with each other in their skill as coachmen, in smartness of appearance, and in the promptness with which the schedules were maintained.

The start of the coaching season became a social occasion, widely reported in the London papers. On one such occasion the Prince of Wales occupied a box seat of the Duke of Beaufort's family coach, and the passengers included the Countess of Westmoreland and Lady Emily Kingscote, the daughters of Lord Curzon. Ironically, it was Lady Emily's husband who was to put Charles into the Court of Chancery where he was threatened with imprisonment for his indiscretions with Beatie Sumner, the niece of the Kingscotes.

As Margaret Hoare's collection of newspaper cuttings grew it came to include, at first by chance, and subsequently by design, the names of people who had two things in common: they came from the Gloucestershire hunting world, and they would one day feature in the scandal that was to break up her marriage. She even meticulously filed reports which hinted not too obscurely at her husband's infidelities.

3 – *Huntsman and Huntress*

Beatie was fifteen when, in 1877, Charles finally abandoned coaching in Kent for the hunting scene in Gloucestershire. Charles was now very rich indeed, having been made a senior partner of Hoare's Bank in London. If his attentions to the girl were to give offence to her father, they were to prove almost as unpalatable to Lord Bathurst, the sixth Earl – and another of Beatie's aristocratic relatives, since both the Earl and her grandfather, William Sumner, had married into the Hankey family of Fetcham Park, Surrey. The Earl, who lived in Cirencester, had welcomed Charles to the county and encouraged him to become Master of the V.W.H. in succession to Lord Shannon. He could not have foreseen that, in the struggle to continue as Master, following the scandalous affair with Beatie, Charles would use his wealth to make virulent attacks on the Earl's own status and fortunes.

In the 1920s the seventh Earl Bathurst wrote a history of the V.W.H. Hunt. Reflecting on the turbulent relationship between his father and Charles Hoare, he said:

It was an unlucky day on which Mr C. A. R. Hoare was elected Master of the V.W.H., for his mastership led to all sorts of social difficulties, as well as extreme friction between land-owners and farmers in the country . . . Mr Hoare was a big, stout, rather common-looking man. He was rich, having been a partner in Hoare's Bank. He set himself up as being a great sportsman, and a coaching man, and probably looked his best in a big box-cloth coat, driving either a four-in-hand, or a pair of horses in a mail phaeton![1]

In a footnote Lord Bathurst added: 'He was nicknamed "The Coachman".'[2]

The 'Coachman's' first home in Gloucestershire was Easton Grey

House, five miles from the Duke of Beaufort's home at Badminton. Kingscote village, where Beatie's uncle, Colonel Nigel Kingscote, lived, was six miles away. The village was at the heart of the Colonel's estate, which was so vast that it included a private race course. Cirencester, the heart of V.W.H. country, was fourteen miles away. Charles's connections in the country were already strong, dating back to his coaching days in London. Yet they were more than merely sporting connections. When the daughter of Henry Van Notten Pole married Reginald Herbert in 1875 the ceremony took place in a church in Fulham Road, London, and the reception at the Ranelagh Club nearby. Bride and groom departed for a honeymoon at Kelsey Park, Beckenham, 'the picturesque and charming seat of Mr C. A. R. Hoare'.[3] Many of those they left behind came from Gloucestershire, and the list of guests was headed by the Duke and Duchess of Beaufort.

There is nothing to suggest that Charles's move to Gloucestershire and his wish to take over the V.W.H. from Lord Shannon were in any way connected with his passion for Beatie Sumner, but being the Master of one of the foremost hunt clubs, in country bordering on that in which Beatie's father was Master, made it easy for the two to meet under the guise of a shared passion for the sport rather than for one another. It may have been chance. Hindsight makes it look like design.

In the run-up to his election as Master, Charles filled the year with activities which were congenial to him but which also served to ingratiate him with the people with whom he was later to come into conflict. He played cricket in Cirencester Park for 'An XI of Cirencester' which included Lord Bathurst ('C. A. R. Hoare *b*. Clark, 3, Earl Bathurst, *c*. Joshua, *b*. Burnett, o').[4] He attended lawn tennis tournaments at the same venue. More than anything, he enjoyed the main events of the hunting calendar – the hunt balls, the opening meetings, the annual dinners and the puppy shows, which were invariably followed by luncheon and formal speeches. Whether

at the King's Head in Cirencester or the Plough Hotel in Cheltenham, he was treated as an honoured guest and his presence duly
recorded in the local papers.

When Charles succeeded Lord Shannon in 1879, he did so on a
wave of goodwill from the whole countryside. Even Arthur Sumner,
in spite of Charles's distressing over-attentiveness to Beatie,
welcomed the new Master to his table and joined cheerfully in a toast
to 'the Neighbouring Hunts' when the Cotswold and the V.W.H.
dined together that year. Sumner returned the visit and attended a
V.W.H. puppy show. It was a wet day. The puppies had been judged,
luncheon served in a marquee next to the Cirencester kennels, and
the prizes awarded. In view of the heavy rain, Charles, as Chairman,
suggested 'a little harmony to pass away the time till the weather saw
fit to mend'.[5] And so the hunt club members sang to each other –
hunting songs and old English ballads. In a lull in the music, Sumner
made an impromptu speech in which he observed amid cheers that it
would be wrong for them to separate without thanking and drinking
the health of their generous and popular host.

However, the shadows were lengthening. That same year, it
became necessary to move Beatie from Cheltenham, so ardent had
Charles become in pursuit of the girl. He was caught in her bedroom
in circumstances which he could not satisfactorily explain. Beatie's
father and her uncle, Colonel Kingscote, brought her and Charles
together and demanded a pledge that they would no longer meet or
communicate with each other in any way. So uncertain were they that
the lovers would honour this pledge that they persuaded Lord and
Lady Fitzhardinge to take Beatie into Berkeley Castle. The castle
was then, as it is now, an unusual and splendid house which had
developed within the walls of a great fortress: there was no suggestion of Beatie being locked up in a tower like the heroine of one of
Mrs Radcliffe's novels nor would Charles Hoare be invited to meet
her there. It was hoped, however, that all her activities could be
monitored more closely in a place which was remote from town life,

where there were no busy streets into which a precocious girl could disappear on her own private errands.

In the world outside the castle, Charles worked hard at building a reputation as the busiest and most extravagant Master the Hunt had ever known. He began by moving to Cirencester, where he took over the lease of the house on Cecily Hill, recently vacated by his predecessor, Lord Shannon. The house stood in a cul-de-sac which was closed off by elegant wrought-iron gates. Beyond them was a five-mile ride, straight as an arrow, across Cirencester Park, the property of Earl Bathurst. In effect, Charles, the Master of the V.W.H., was living a stone's throw from the home of the Chairman, whose house was on the edge of the town, screened from it by grey walls and the highest yew hedge in the world. Occasionally, Master and Chairman would start a day's hunting at the most convenient point imaginable – outside Cecily Hill House itself, with the vast acreage of the Park, superb hunting country, inviting beyond the iron gates. The hounds had barely a mile to come from their kennels on the Tetbury Road, along the path which passed by the lake, and across the front of Lord Bathurst's house where it lay in a hollow with the tower of Cirencester parish church rearing up behind – though too far from it for anyone to see more than its roof and top storey.

Charles planned to hunt six days a week and, for that purpose, built up three separate packs. In fact he hunted five days with the V.W.H. and went out with the Badminton on Monday, which was market day in Cirencester, where most of his followers had business.

Whatever his failings, it could not be denied that Charles, now in his early thirties, was a man of immense energy who relished hunting as – in the words of Mr Jorrocks – 'the sport of kings, the image of war without its guilt, and only five-and-twenty per cent of its danger'. The hunting world around Cirencester was light years away from the decks of the *Mercury*, but when Charles made the leap from one to the other, he imposed a hardy and strenuous life on the boys in his care with the ease of a man who had known as much himself – and rejoiced in it.

As Charles's fortunes were waxing in Cirencester, those of Arthur Sumner in the neighbouring Cotswold country were on the decline. Lord Fitzhardinge chaired a meeting in the Plough Hotel, Cheltenham, at which the Hunt secretary read out the sorry details of declining membership, overdue subscriptions and increasing costs. Remedies were suggested, such as getting landowners to do the earth-stopping themselves, thus saving £240 a year, and the creation of a committee of farmers to superintend and pay poultry bills out of a special fund for the purpose. Sumner was to be spared the cost of providing luncheon at the hunt puppy shows, the kind of event which Charles in Cirencester was turning into a gala affair of unbelievable opulence, all paid for from his apparently bottomless pocket.[6]

As for Mrs Hoare, she was settling into Cirencester life, untouched as yet by the differing fortunes of the two local Masters of Foxhounds, and unaware that they were to prove major ingredients in the troubles that lay ahead. She busied herself with the social and cultural life of the locality. On Thursday, 13 November 1879, she appeared in a 'Grand Amateur Concert' given in Cirencester Corn Hall, the proceeds from which were 'to be devoted to the Objects of the Temperance Cause in Cirencester'.[7] She went to Chippenham to attend a fine arts exhibition at the New Hall, in which 700 items were put on display, some from her own home. Amongst the visitors to the exhibition were Beatie's relatives, the Duchess of Beaufort and Lady Fitzhardinge.

Beatie, languishing in the seclusion of Berkeley Castle, should have been cut off from the events in Cirencester, but her descendants are not so sure of this. The culprit, they believe, was a close relation. In July of that year her cousin, Winifred Ida, a daughter of Colonel Kingscote, had married Lord Rocksavage, who was later to become the Marquess of Cholmondeley. The latter was nineteen and his bride seventeen, three months older than Beatie. As a married woman, Winifred could now walk with a 'larger tether', and it is possible that Charles enlisted her to carry messages into the castle and arrange assignations. Later, he found another ally in Major Fitzhardinge Kingscote, known to his intimates as Fitz.

Fitz was Colonel Kingscote's half-brother. He had been born in 1837, and had joined the army in 1854. In November of that year, still only seventeen, he was promoted from ensign to lieutenant. It was the time of the Crimean War, and the two half-brothers were in the campaign, Fitz as a dashing young officer in the thick of the fighting, and Nigel, nearly ten years his senior, on Lord Raglan's staff; Nigel sent home a stream of letters describing the war, and in one of them he mentioned his encounter with a soldier in the same regiment as Fitz:

I want to tell you a speech one of the 41st made who was lying in bed wounded at the sanatorium. I asked him if he knew Fitzhardinge Kingscote, not telling him who I was myself. He answered in an Irish accent, 'Sure I do, a fine young gentleman he is. Faith I would go with him anywhere. He don't care one bit for shot and shell.'

Very complimentary was it not?[8]

With his disregard for the ironmongery of war, Fitz collected an injury which nearly killed him. His right hand was smashed in the fighting at the Radan, and he spent a night lost in the open. When he was found in the morning, he had almost bled to death. Nigel heard of it and got his brother moved to a hospital near Raglan's headquarters, but he could do nothing to allay the suffering that followed. In his diary Fitz told of three attempts by the surgeons to get above the gangrene in the wound, sawing at the mutilated stump with the patient fully conscious in spite of crude attempts at anaesthetising him with chloroform. For the rest of his life he wore a hook where his right hand should have been. He stayed in the army, becoming a captain in 1856, and attaining the rank of major before he retired in 1868. Along the way he served in Canada, India and Ireland. In Canada, he met and married Agnes Grant Stuart, and when he left the army they settled in Ireland, where they had eight children and made a precarious living, renting property in the country and taking in paying guests who came for the hunting. England, however, was still home, and he made frequent visits, staying with relatives in Gloucestershire.

When Charles pressed him into service, Fitz's financial difficulties were becoming acute. In early middle age he was still handsome, though he confessed to his diary that he had his hair tinted bronze. He was a charming, genial man, who had proved himself to be brave almost to the point of madness, and would hunt over the wildest country with his one good hand.

Beatie emerged from Berkeley Castle early in 1881 with those responsible for keeping her there harbouring a strong suspicion that the exercise had been a waste of time. She had had access to horses and was such a superb horsewoman that few could keep up with her if she left the castle for a ride over the Gloucestershire countryside. Short of locking her in her rooms there was really no way in which her guardians could prevent her from making contact with Charles, and in March of that year the eighteen-year-old Beatie conspired to spend over four months in Charles's house on Cecily Hill, sleeping in a room directly over that occupied by his wife. The latter pasted four newspaper cuttings into her leather-bound scrapbook which indicated how this was achieved, and what followed after. The first two describe an incident during a meet of the V.W.H. near Barnsley, a village four miles out of Cirencester on the road to Burford:

Accident to Miss Sumner. On Tuesday March 1st a somewhat serious accident happened to Miss Sumner, daughter of Captain Sumner, Master of the Cotswold Hounds. The accomplished equestrienne joined a party in the meet of the V.W.H. Hounds at Barnsley. In the course of a hot run she was negotiating a difficult fence – a stone stile with a ditch on the taking off side, when her horse made a mistake, slipped into the grip, and threw the fair rider violently upon her head and shoulders. As quickly as possible a conveyance was procured and the sufferer brought into the residence of Mr C. A. R. Hoare, where she was attended by a medical gentleman and found not to be seriously injured as was at first supposed. Captain Sumner subsequently arrived and stopped with his daughter for some days.[9]

The second report differs in only one detail, saying that 'Captain Sumner subsequently arrived and stayed in the town'.[10]

Her descendants are in little doubt as to what really happened on that day. Beatie was not thrown when her horse made a mistake: she deliberately threw herself to the ground. She faked the whole business, with Charles's connivance, so that she could gain a means of entry to his house, and her questionable injury provided the excuse for her stay there.

Chatcomb was the setting for the next act. What took place is summarised in the third of Margaret Hoare's cuttings:

Monday, the 7th. Cotswold at Chatcomb. A big muster, including Captain Sumner and Miss Sumner (who I very much regret to hear met with an accident out with the V.W.H. Hounds on Tuesday last, when her horse fell and rolled on her. She was taken at once to Cirencester, where medical assistance was obtained, and I feel assured I only echo the sentiments of all connected with the Hunting in this neighbourhood by saying I sincerely trust she is not seriously hurt and that we shall see her in the saddle again), Mr C. Hoare . . .[11]

the list goes on with another two dozen names of the principal Hunt members.

Charles hunted that day, and Beatie watched from his carriage, and returned – disconcertingly – not to her own home a mere three miles away in Cheltenham, but to her 'sick-bed' in Cecily Hill House, Cirencester, twelve miles in the opposite direction.

In April, a newspaper published the last of the four items bracketed together by Mrs Hoare: 'Miss Sumner is still confined to her bed at Cirencester in consequence of the spinal injury she received at the time of her accident in the hunting field a month ago.'[12] So blatant was the impropriety that Beatie's father could not ignore it and, in July, he approached Charles directly and upbraided him for his dishonourable conduct. Charles admitted it, as did Beatie: there was not very much else they could do. They both wept bitterly.[13] It was a touching scene which might have mitigated the harsher judgements of those outside Cecily Hill House had they been witness to it – the big man of the hunting world and a young girl, helpless in the face of their passion for each other. Sumner kept his counsel for a few more years, but to begin with he had to devise yet another plan to keep the two apart.

Incarcerating Beatie in Berkeley Castle had proved a failure. The next gambit was to have recourse to the law. On 20 December 1881 Beatie was made a ward of court, her status in law being that of an infant. Injunctions were served on her and Charles restraining them from having any intercourse or communication, direct or indirect.[14] At first they tried rather feebly to obey the injunctions, but in June 1882 there began a series of events which made the court order hardly worth the paper on which it was written.

Beatie's father was in desperate financial difficulties. He faced bankruptcy, the most galling immediate result of which was the seizure of his horses. Mrs Sumner, casting about her for a source of money to stave off the disaster facing them, persuaded Beatie to approach Lord Rocksavage for the loan of £200. Lord Rocksavage, the newest member of the family since his marriage to Beatie's cousin Winifred, declined to help, even though Beatie was sent twice to London to appeal to him. On her return to Cheltenham from the second of these journeys, she immediately informed her mother, who persuaded her to telegraph Lord Rocksavage asking yet again for the money. This time it was forthcoming, and Mrs Sumner used it to settle her own debts. Informing her mother of the result of her interview with Lord Rocksavage, Beatie suggested Charles as a source of funds. To begin with, Mrs Sumner upbraided her daughter's wickedness at putting such temptation before her, but by the following morning she had made up her mind. To save her husband she was going to write to Charles and ask him for a loan of £3000 – a figure slightly larger than her husband's actual debts. The letter written, she asked Beatie to read it before sending her out to post it. As she explained much later and in extenuation, she could not give it to a servant, and she was not going out herself.[15]

Charles's reply came back, offering cash, but only on condition that Mr Sumner was fully informed about what was happening. Mr Sumner, however, was not at home, and had not been for some time. He was at Cranford House, staying with Lord Fitzhardinge. Beatie and her mother consulted the family solicitor, a Mr Chesshyre, about the feasibility of borrowing money from the man with whom Beatie was forbidden to communicate, and a way was found for the transaction to take place. Mrs Sumner sent for her husband, explained the position, and in due course and with his full approval the money was formally applied for and delivered. Mrs Sumner, who had a rather prosaic notion of how financial transactions were conducted, had originally asked for '£3000 – she wouldn't settle for less – cash, in a lump, in an envelope'.[16] The transfer through the office of Mr Chesshyre was less crudely achieved. It did, however, give rise to the story, which persisted for over a hundred years, that Charles had bought Beatie from her parents for the sum of £3000.

Their financial problems eased, Mrs Sumner at once arranged a trip to Germany with her daughter. Something of her ineffectuality, her tendency to rely on Beatie's organising abilities, is demonstrated by the fact that she asked her daughter to invite Major Kingscote, Beatie's Uncle Fitz, to accompany them, and for the next two years he was almost constantly at hand.

Before their departure in mid-July 1882, Beatie – a budding casuist – persuaded her uncle to ask his solicitor, a Mr Inderwick, if it would be possible for two people, kept apart by a court order in England, to meet abroad.[17] The solicitor's reply was unequivocal: yes, two such people could meet, but no, they would never be able to return to England again without answering to the law. The law applied no matter where they went.

Even though the grave consequences of any breach of the court order had been spelled out to him, Fitz took up the task of keeping

43

Charles and Beatie in touch. He was in debt to Charles, from whom
he had begun to borrow earlier that year, leaving his carriage as
security. He wrote from Weilbad, where they were staying in
Germany, asking for further loans, and persuaded Beatie to include
her letters in the same envelopes as a safeguard against detection.
Charles could always say that he had never knowingly received a
letter from Beatie for the simple reason that her handwriting never
appeared on the envelope.[18]

They returned to London in September, and Fitz took Beatie to
the home of her widowed aunt, Mrs Martin, at 20 Seymour Street.
Unknown to them, Mrs Martin's butler, James Kennelly, had
already begun collecting the kind of evidence which would prove so
damaging when the lovers appeared in court in 1885. In July, just
before their departure to Germany, Kennelly had answered the door
when a cabman came to collect Beatie, declaring that Mr Hoare had
sent him. Kennelly took the cabman's number, 8592, and told all in
an affidavit in May 1884.[19]

Beatie had presents for Charles – a whip and a stick she had
bought in Germany – so her uncle arranged a meeting between them
at the Great Western Hotel in Paddington. Fitz took the presents
into the hotel, leaving Beatie in the cab, but Charles, mature and
discreet, refused to accept them and steeled himself not to see Beatie
even when Fitz told him she was crying in the cab outside.[20]

From Seymour Street Beatie went to Cholmondeley Castle in
Cheshire, where her cousin, Lady Rocksavage, took up the task of
keeping alive the correspondence with Charles. During the month
she spent at the castle forays were made to London and Gloucestershire, with Fitz trying to get Charles and Beatie to meet. On one
occasion, Fitz and his niece were on the same train as Charles, but in
different compartments. When it stopped at Swindon, Fitz tried to
persuade Charles to come into the same compartment as them, but
he ran out of the station, leaving Beatie in tears.

In October a second trip abroad began. This time there were four in the party after another uncle, Edgar Hanbury, had joined them. They stayed in Paris, visiting the Louvre and Notre Dame, and attending the theatre in the evening. Fitz kept his diary, and recorded their stays in Bologna, Florence, Rome and Milan. In Florence there was a drama when a telegram arrived to warn Fitz that criminal proceedings were being instituted against him for reasons unspecified, but probably owing to unpaid debts. He would have to find £200 to avert this, and there was a flurry of messages between Beatie, the solicitor Inderwick and Charles – the latter being pressed into providing the money so that the holiday could go on uninterrupted, and Beatie insisting that she did not want to go home merely to attend to her uncle's legal problems.[21] Their pleasures were unremarkable and consisted of the conventional English tourist round – cathedrals and art galleries by day, the theatre in the evenings. They were never enthusiastic about what they saw, never moved to comment favourably or otherwise on the entertainments they found; Fitz recorded in his diary the simple fact that they had gone to the theatre, seldom bothering to specify whether it were to see a play or an opera.

After their return to London in November, Beatie moved into 31 Halsey Street, Cadogan Square, where she was in the care of a Madame Mosson, who was employed by Colonel Kingscote specifically for the purpose.

On 12 July 1883, Beatie celebrated her twenty-first birthday by going to the offices of Inderwick with Charles to ask if there was anything in law to prevent them living together. There were no obstacles apart from moral ones, the solicitor assured them.[22] For six years the two had defied all attempts at separating them. The rules for the upbringing of a young Victorian lady of 'good' family had hardly applied to the defiant, spirited Beatie, who wanted her own way in everything. In fact her singularity can hardly be stressed enough.

She had two sisters who went through the careful grooming appropriate to their class and married well – Madelaine to Sir

George Banks Jenkinson, and Gertrude to Admiral Heaton-Ellis – but she would have none of it. There was no 'coming out' for her, no presentation at Court in spite of her powerful connections with the Royal Family. So extreme was her attitude that it takes no more than a little amateur psychology to predict that, in the event of her ever relenting, she would be the victim of a sort of psychological inversion. Indiscipline would be intolerable in others when she reflected on the harm it had done in her own life. Sexual phenomena would become distasteful to a woman who had once been ruled by her desires. The sexuality perhaps of her children, certainly of the boys she was eventually to rule, would be crushed by no more elaborate devices than driving them to the point of exhaustion every day of their lives, and by keeping them so hungry that they had no interest but in food and sleep.

For a while after her coming of age Beatie continued to live with Madame Mosson. Her Uncle Fitz returned to his wife and children in Galway, but was back in England on 3 August, when he dined with Beatie and Charles at Halsey Street and then accompanied them to Drury Lane Theatre to see the first night performance of a play entitled *Freedom* by G. F. Rowe and Augustus Harris.

The following day they went to stay at the Granville Hotel, Ramsgate, with Uncle Fitz once again in his role as chaperone. Madame Mosson had disappeared on holiday for a few weeks. Fitz was certain that nothing improper took place between his two companions, at least not while they were in Ramsgate. He could not be held responsible for them when they went up to London on 28 September, returning the following day. They felt obliged to explain to him where they had slept – Beatie in the empty house in Halsey Street, and Charles at 37 Fleet Street, the premises of the Hoare Bank.[23] None the less, their first child was born nine months later on 23 June 1884. She was christened Sybil. Sixty-one years later she sat with her mother and listened to the sounds drifting from the ship in the middle of the Hamble River.

There seemed little point in concealing their relationship, and the services of Madame Mosson – met off the ferry at Dover at the beginning of October – were swiftly dispensed with. Fitz was sent to Faringdon in Berkshire to look at a shooting box, Wicklesham Lodge, the property of a Colonel Edwards who was abroad on military service. Mr Adams of Faringdon acted as the Colonel's landlord. The house, much extended in recent years, stands on a lonely hilltop site which, in the 1880s, was approached by a long narrow drive that came up almost from Faringdon itself, a mile and a half away. From the house one can see the town and the squat square tower of the parish church near the market place. Coincidence can at times astonish, but presumably the modern owner of the lodge who placed a statue of the god Mercury on the lawn outside the southern windows, was unaware that this was the first home of Charles and Beatie, the man who founded a school of the same name, and the woman who eventually ran it.

4 – The Gloucestershire Scandal

The hunting season of 1883–4 was one of frantic activity on the part of Charles. When it began, Beatie was pregnant and the household at Faringdon was the subject of gossip that found its way into the London weekly papers, with sly references in *Vanity Fair* and *Truth* to 'the uncle . . . who makes an admirable chaperone'. Margaret Hoare diligently cut these out and put them in her scrapbook.[1]

In November, at the start of the season, Lord Fitzhardinge, Colonel Nigel Kingscote and Mr Sumner descended on Inderwick at the solicitor's offices in London, imploring him to put pressure on those at Faringdon to break up a household which they felt was too outrageous to be tolerated.[2] Inderwick tried letters and telegrams without success, addressing them mainly to Fitzhardinge Kingscote, who simply passed them on to Charles. The latter, disenchanted with Inderwick for taking the side of the Kingscote and Sumner families, took his legal problems elsewhere.

The level of Inderwick's desperation comes through in the tone of one of his letters: 'Dear Fitz, For God's sake come and see me. I want to do you a turn if you will only let me . . .'[3]. Charles's wealth was such that he could have retired to any one of half-a-dozen large houses which he either owned or rented, and let the uproar over his relationship with Beatie burn itself out. It would not have been the first time a man of his position had taken such a course, but he seemed compelled to justify his position, to prove to society that he was indifferent to its opinions. To continue in public life meant continuing in the role of Master of the V.W.H. and, without being particularly prescient, he could see that, for social reasons, the club would sooner or later decide that his conduct was insupportable. He

48

had, as it were, carried off a most promising scion of one of the best connected families in Gloucestershire, a girl who was welcome in all the great houses – Badminton, Cirencester Park, Berkeley Castle and many more – as a respected relative of the people there. Lord Bathurst, the Chairman of the V.W.H., had made his position plain early in the season. Arthur Sumner approached him and complained about the ménage at Faringdon of Charles, Beatie and her Uncle Fitz. Lord Bathurst wrote to Charles asking for his version of events, and received assurances that the rumours circulating in the country were utterly false. Charles even called on Lord Bathurst to reinforce his story, but the noble lord would not accept it, saying that 'we must be on different terms from those on which we have hitherto met.'[4]

Charles found his supporters among his tenant farmers. They were in the middle of an agricultural depression as farm prices reached rock bottom in the face of cheap grain imported from the newly opened prairies of North America. Many were reduced to subsistence living, and, when they abandoned their farms, the landlords in turn felt the pinch as they could not find new tenants. In Charles, the tenant farmers felt that they had found a champion who was rich and was on their side, opposed to the landlords. He plied them with money, food, entertainment, horses, loans, gifts of all kinds but, above all, with sport – hunting conducted with vigour and on a scale unheard of in the entire history of the V.W.H. country. Charles almost lived in the saddle. That season he hunted his hounds on 144 days, killed 82 brace, and ran 15 brace of foxes to ground.[5] On 22 December 1883, there began one of those epic hunts, the details of which are pored over ever after by the followers of the sport. It was the kind of event which made people indulgent towards the man who made it possible, conveniently obscuring for many the details of his personal life.

The hunt was dubbed 'The Great Crouch Run' after the place where it started, and the reports of it, at the time, were so complete that today one could use them to go over the same ground almost field by field. A writer in the *Wilts and Gloucestershire Standard* came close to capturing the excitement of the event, but not the courage and stamina of huntsmen and women, horses and hounds thundering across nearly thirty miles of country almost non-stop. Nor did he capture the sheer weariness at the end of the thirty-mile journey home, as they climbed the fingerposts in the dark to find the right way.[6]

In spite of the sport he offered, it became clear to Charles that the hunt would soon be split between his supporters and those surrounding Lord Bathurst, and he began laying his plans against that day. He initiated a railway service on one day a week which would take hounds, servants and horses from Cirencester to Swindon. Any members who wished to do so could take the train and be in Swindon before lunch, have a good afternoon out, and catch another train back in time for dinner. In his obituary Charles was described as 'opening the Swindon country',[7] as if the Master had set about doing the hunting world a particular favour by bringing the sport to an area where it had previously been lacking. There was no altruism in this bit of organisation. Rather it served to create a stronghold for Charles, an area in which tenant farmers through their sheer numbers would keep him in the field if there were demands for his resignation. The agricultural depression once again served his purpose, enabling him to reinforce his grip on the country by renting huge blocks of land, ostensibly for the shooting, but in fact in order to limit the operations of a rival pack.

By February 1884, his popularity was such that his public appearances were greeted by crowds with banners. A journalist reporting a meet at Ashton Keynes digressed from his description of the day's sport to tell of the reception provided in the village for the 'popular Master of the Vale Hounds':

Never in the whole course of my life have I witnessed anything at all like it. It put me in mind of a general election more than anything else. Flags were displayed, mottoes posted up, and painted in very conspicuous letters, and so arranged that they must have been seen by nearly every individual out that day. They were as follows: 'Success to our M.F.H. and his supporters' – 'Mr Hoare the Farmers' Friend. Long may he stay with us – Tally-ho'. 'A divided pack spoils sport' – 'Success to Mr Hoare' – 'Hoare for ever'. These mottoes were to be seen at different places, commencing at North End, and extending to the centre of the village, a distance of over half a mile.[8]

The reference to the divided pack was a sign that the public had by now gathered that such a possibility was on the cards, with more and more people in Lord Bathurst's circle refusing to appear in the field with Charles while the household at Faringdon was in being.

In spite of the situation at Wicklesham Lodge, Mrs Hoare put a brave face on things and appeared in public with her husband, often arriving in her carriage to see the hunt assemble at the start of a day in the field.[9] But behind the scenes the façade was beginning to crack. Fitzhardinge Kingscote was getting letters from his half-brother Nigel, telling him of the Kingscote family's disgust at his behaviour. Fitz, however, was so dependent on allowances from Charles that he could not break out of the trap that Wicklesham had become for him. At last he wrote to Inderwick, begging to be released:

Faringdon
3 January '84

Dear Mr Inderwick,
    I am willing at once to change my way of life and go to Galway and remain there and estrange myself altogether from my present companions if you can get me the sum of £100 to pay the debts I have contracted in the last few months since I had no regular allowance – also if you are paid what you expended for me and I am guaranteed my fixed regular monthly allowance – If these three things can be arranged I can at once break up this establishment and leave England and end the Scandal –

Yrs sincerely
F. Kingscote[10]

Fitz, of course, was mistaken in thinking that the scandal was rooted in his presence at Wicklesham and that his departure would end it. He took his departure, but when he reached Galway he found that his wife had been kept informed of the situation in England, and in less than two years this handsome, gentle woman, still in her early forties, had gone white-haired with worry.

Back in V.W.H. country, the fight between landlords and tenantry – for that is what it had become – grew more intense. When men on the landlords' side refused to speak to him at a meet, Charles threatened to take the hounds back to kennels, and when, as expected, a call for his resignation was made; his admirers gathered six hundred signatures purporting to be those of the tenant farmers who were on his side. The signatures were appended to what was described as a 'memorial', which was little more than a veiled threat, demanding the withdrawal of the request for Charles's resignation, while implying that by their sheer weight of numbers they would make it impossible for anyone to hunt, whether landlords or tenants. The Hunt Committee decided 'to waive their own views in deference to so strong and general expression of opinion and . . . directed a communication to that effect to be directed to Mr Hoare'.[11]

Charles's victory was to be shortlived. As early as March 1884, he was warned of an action being prepared against him for contempt of court for having, in breach of the court order of December 1881, 'had communication . . . with Beatrice Holme Sumner'.

The action gained momentum in May when, on the 14th, Fitzhardinge Kingscote was traced to Glenina in County Galway, and persuaded to make an affidavit in which he gave details of nearly two years he had spent with Beatie and Charles.[12] A fortnight later solicitors interviewed James Kennelly,[13] the butler at 20 Seymour Street, and Robert Blott, formerly a servant at the Norfolk Square Hotel, but by this time one of the crew of the SS *Prins Hendrik*.[14] Kennelly obligingly told them about the cabman, and Blott about his duties in the hotel rooms Charles had occupied at weekends earlier that year when he was visited by a lady called Miss Hoare. He was shown photos of Beatie and identified her as the lady.

Charles was sufficiently alarmed by these proceedings to file his own affidavit on 5 June – eleven pages and twenty-seven paragraphs, in which he tried to anticipate all the charges likely to be made against him.[15] Fitzhardinge Kingscote was blamed for persistently trying to get him to communicate with Beatie, and it was revealed that Charles had loaned him £750; nothing was said about his loan of £3000 to the Sumners. Wicklesham Lodge was not referred to except in such a way as to make Inderwick's desperate efforts to bring to an end the arrangements there in November of the previous year appear impertinent.

Now more than ever Charles needed friends. The Hoare family had left Cecily Hill House and moved to the Querns, an equally spacious place further away from Lord Bathurst's house but still convenient to the kennels; and on 13 August, two months after Sybil's birth, the annual hunt puppy show was held there.[16] Hunt members were there to watch the judging of the puppies at the kennels. These were the animals born the previous year which had been farmed out to 'puppy walkers', people who would look after them from the time they were weaned until they were old and robust enough to be introduced to the pack. As always on these occasions, there was lunch for everybody, Charles paying for food and wine served in a marquee which had been erected in the grounds of the Querns. Margaret supervised the catering arrangements and lunched with the company. With the other ladies present, she withdrew when the time came for toasts and speeches.

Charles took the chair. He got to his feet and began a long, rambling and sycophantic speech to an audience composed predominantly of tenant farmers. He began with a toast to the Queen, and said he was anxious to get through the official and customary toasts, which it was one's duty as well as one's pleasure to propose, as quickly as he could.

Further toasts followed: to the Prince of Wales (who had once hunted with the Cirencester pack), to the Church – not usually responded to at such events, but on this occasion redeemed by the presence in the audience of a clergyman – to the judges, the hunt servants and so forth. There was one salient omission. The Master announced that he would like to drink the health of Earl Bathurst – but added pointedly that a toast afforded little amusement if there was no one there to respond.

The tenant farmers winked at each other in anticipation of the last toast, the formulation of which demonstrated all Charles's skill as a propagandist: he had to propose it, though he dared say he might get into hot water over it. He would be the most ungrateful man in all England if he did not do so and drink heartily, almost to excess, to the tenant farmers and others of this country (*cheers*). Why it had not come first on the list was that he feared it might appear selfish on his part if he did so. It was a toast which he felt very much bound up in, for a good many things had occurred which proved to him how extremely tight was the knot which was tied between him and the country, evidenced by the support which had always been extended to him by the tenant farmers (*loud cheers*). He would not make a long speech to them, it was not his design to set class against class but merely to show by a few wretched miserable words of his how grateful he was to the tenant farmers and others who had met him there, and were not afraid or ashamed to put their names on paper and say 'That is a man we like' (*loud cheering*). They had acted unflinchingly, and he thanked the tenant farmers and others most extremely for the way they had stuck to him, and he could only say that as long as ever he could do so he should stick to them (*loud cheers*). There followed a great deal more in the same vein. An additional, though unlooked-for piece of good luck occurred after-wards, when a farmer got to his feet and declared that, as to the tenant farmers of that hunt, he was not afraid to say in that company that there were very few but would do what they did before – stick to Mr Hoare through thick and thin (*loud cheers*). He thought that the tenant farmers were very few that would go to the other party, who wanted to roll them up and do as they liked with them. But they were not jam pies yet (*cheers and laughter*). He hoped the tenant farmers would stick the same as they did last year, fearless and careless of anyone (*cheers*). There were some ominous remarks about the facility with which tenants could pick and choose their landlords in these changing times. That put a different colour on things. He was much obliged to Mr Hoare for proposing the health of the tenant farmers, and he hoped he would do so for many years to come as Master of the V.W.H. (*loud cheers*). One or two noble faces grew very glum.

Somebody else proposed the health of Mrs Hoare and the ladies who had adorned their table that day, and Charles responded, saying that 'there was no man in this world whose duty it was more to thank them for drinking Mrs Hoare's health'. He said he would not make a long speech, but would simply say one word which comprehended it all, she was 'a woman of a thousand' (*loud cheers*).[17]

Charles's stock rose enormously in the county after this. It declined somewhat, however, seven months later, when he attended the Court of Chancery in London and heard proclaimed

a motion on behalf of Colonel Kingscote for the committal to prison of Charles Arthur Richard Hoare for contempt in having disobeyed an injunction of the Court, dated December 20, 1881, restraining him from having any intercourse, or communication, directly or indirectly, with Miss Beatrice Holme Sumner, who was then an infant, but attained her full age on July 12th 1883, and also forbidding Miss Sumner to have any intercourse or communication with Mr Hoare.[18]

5 – The Judgement

On 17 March 1885, Charles and Beatie came to the Court of Chancery to hear their eight-year-long affair publicly unravelled. The best counsel were on hand, twelve altogether, to represent the different parties. Seven were Q.C.s, including the Attorney-General, Sir Henry James. On the bench was Mr Justice Chitty.[1]

Before them were the affidavits of the people involved. Beatie's ran to eleven substantial pages.[2] Some of its paragraphs were reported verbatim in *The Times* and in the Gloucestershire papers. The £3000 loan, including Beatie's mother's request for 'cash, in a lump, in an envelope', was described. She elaborated on the trips abroad. Of her uncle's involvement she said that 'my mother told me to ask my Uncle, Major Fitzhardinge Kingscote, to accompany us on the plea that he would be a companion to me and that it would be beneficial to him to get him out of England as he was behaving in a disgraceful way . . .'[3] She implicated the Major, her cousin, Winifred Ida, now the Marchioness of Cholmondeley, and her cousin's husband, in the business of communicating with Charles.

The affidavit of the Marchioness, whose husband had acceded to the title of Marquess the previous year, told an entirely different story of having struggled to show Beatie the error of her ways and keep her away from Charles.[4] There was an affidavit from Inderwick,[5] protesting that Charles had interfered with a key witness, the cab driver who had called at the house in Seymour Street to collect Beatie: the cabbie, Thomas Aldous, had been due at Inderwick's office one Sunday, promising to give a good deal of incriminating evidence about Charles and Beatie, and when he

56

failed to arrive there was a strong suspicion that Charles had bribed him not to attend.

Colonel Nigel Kingscote, who had brought the case to court, was only marginally less damaging than Beatie in his revelations of what had happened while his niece had been a ward of court and thereafter. He touched on the arrangements at Wicklesham Lodge, Faringdon, and remarked on 'the considerable scandal . . . created in the Hunting field by the conspicuous attentions of Mr Hoare to the Plaintiff'.[6]

The most strikingly worded document was that submitted by Arthur Randall Huitt, 'Gentleman and Solicitor of the High Court of Justice', in which he stated that

On the ninth day of March 1885, I served the Right Honourable the Marquess of Cholmondeley and the Right Honourable the Marchioness of Cholmondeley of Higginsfield in the County of Chester with a notice in writing instituted in this Action addressed respectively to the said Marquess of Cholmondeley and Marchioness of Cholmondeley and purporting to be a Notice of Motion to be made to Mr Justice Chitty herein for the committal to Prison of them the said Marquess of Cholmondeley and Marchioness of Cholmondeley by delivering a true copy of the said notice . . .[7]

It may have been a mere form of words, in which the court asserted its authority over those who were among the highest in the land, as much as over the humblest cab driver or hotel servant involved in the case, but they were words that were to come perilously close to being enacted.

All but one of the protagonists were in court.[8] The Marquess and Marchioness of Cholmondeley sat in fear of what the day might hold for them. Mr and Mrs Sumner steeled themselves against the moment when their weakness in the face of their daughter's excesses would be revealed. The Earl Bathurst was there in response to a subpoena summoning him to appear as a witness in the case. Nearby was a small band of witnesses from London – a housekeeper, a cabman, the butler from Seymour Street, and hotel servants, among them Robert Blott, who would have things to say which would help plot the twists and turns of an extraordinary affair. Colonel Nigel Kingscote was present – a man who had spent over forty years in the Royal Household as Groom-in-Waiting to Queen Victoria and later as Equerry to the Prince of Wales. Only the colonel's half-brother, 'Uncle Fitz', was missing. He was said to be untraceable, presumably having gone to Ireland to be well out of the way, for he knew that his presence there would be disastrous to many people. Sadly, in his absence, there is every indication that he was used as a scapegoat, someone who could be vilified freely since he was in no position to defend himself.

The proceedings opened with Mr Ince Q.C., in support of the motion, saying that Colonel Kingscote's position was simply that of a trustee in whom a fund had been invested for the purpose of protecting Miss Sumner, and that he felt it to be his duty to bring forward the facts of the case and leave the matter in the hands of the court.

Mr Charles Russell Q.C., on behalf of Miss Sumner, objected to the motion being opened at all. Miss Sumner was now twenty-three years of age. She was in fact no party to the motion, and she disclaimed proceedings which could no longer be said to be taken for her protection or in her interest, but rather to be actuated by private motives. On her behalf he protested emphatically against proceedings which could only be prejudicial to her interests.

When Charles's counsel, Mr Davey Q.C., got to his feet, the court might have expected an opening shot along the same formal lines as those used by Ince and Russell, protesting his client's innocence, perhaps, or at least reaffirming the point already made – that Beatie was no longer a ward of court, and that the motives of Colonel Kingscote in bringing the case were questionable. He began, however, by objecting to the reading of affidavits which, he said, contained merely hearsay evidence; no evidence could be admitted except that which was within the strictest rules of admissibility.

When Mr Ince rose to announce that he would read Major Kingscote's affidavit, Davey was on his feet again, protesting loudly. He knew that if Charles Hoare was going to end up in prison this was the document that would see it effected.

'Is Major Kingscote here to be cross-examined?' asked Davey.

'You know well enough why he is not here,' said Ince, piqued at this reminder that the one witness who could help his client's case could not be found.

Mr Justice Chitty said he would hear the affidavit, adding wearily, 'I fail to see the value of this fencing.'

Still on the defensive, Davey objected in advance to any evidence that was not to do with the period under discussion – the eighteen months during which Beatie was a ward of court. He knew only too well what was coming: not just the details of the irregularities during that period, the lovers constantly in touch through the busy offices of Fitz and the then Lady Rocksavage, but the aftermath, the precipitate manner in which they had gone to Inderwick to seek assurances that the law could not touch them if they decided to live together openly. There would be the matter of Beatie's pregnancy, and the household at Faringdon would be mentioned along with the other addresses she had stayed at – Halsey Street, Seymour Street, and another in St. John's Wood. All this on top of earlier extravagances, trips to the Continent and an opulent life in London of theatres and dining out, would destroy his client. At some point the question of 'Who had paid for all this?' would be asked. Not bankrupt Mr Sumner, that was certain, nor Fitz Kingscote with his tenuous grip on solvency, nor Colonel Kingscote with his 'fund invested for the purpose of protecting Miss Sumner'. It had to be Charles Hoare, senior partner in the bank of the same name. For Davey there loomed the prospect of his client going to prison, with the corollary that those who had abetted him would go too. Charles, Beatie, her cousin Lady Cholmondeley, Fitz Kingscote, and Mr and Mrs Sumner stood in a row like dominoes: if one fell the whole lot would go, and what had been a minor provincial scandal would explode beyond the bounds of Chancery into the Royal court, with two of Her Majesty's closest and most trusted servants, the Marquess of Cholmondeley and Colonel Kingscote, embarrassed by the public humiliation of erring relatives.

Major Kingscote's affidavit was read, but it was not until Mr Justice Chitty delivered his judgement that Davey learned with relief that only those parts were admissible which had been corroborated by witnesses present in the court.

The minor *dramatis personae* took the stage. A servant who had seen Beatie and Charles at the Great Western Hotel identified them when they were ordered to stand up for his inspection. Robert Blott – fetched off his ship to give evidence – answered questions about meetings in the Norfolk Square Hotel. Thomas Aldous, the cab driver who had been spotted by James Kennelly at Seymour Street, provided a little light relief. He began by demanding his expenses since his cab was being kept waiting (*laughter*). He said he never was in the service of Lord Cholmondeley. Lord Cholmondeley was formerly Rocksavage. His (Thomas Aldous's) acquaintance lay amongst noblemen (*laughter*). It did not include Mr Hoare (*more laughter*). He knew Miss Sumner. In 1883 he saw her in Sloane Street, and afterwards she gave him orders to drive her. He used to give that lady his account, and she used to pay him. He very seldom drove Miss Sumner alone. She was usually accompanied by one of her own sex. She was sometimes accompanied by a gentleman.

Bit by bit the stratagems Charles and Beatie had used in order to communicate with each other were exposed. The court learned of the extraordinary lengths Colonel Kingscote and Mr Sumner had gone to to keep them apart, including the period in which they tried to confine Beatie to Berkeley Castle under the eyes of Lord and Lady Fitzhardinge. The 'accident in the hunting field', which led to four months of amorous dalliance while Beatie was still in her teens, was described in detail. One can only guess at the bewilderment of those in court when it transpired that these people, who had striven so diligently to keep the banker and the girl apart, had gone on to borrow money from the one at the suggestion of the other.

Charles was cross-examined by Mr Ince and had, predictably, to answer questions about the possibility of his having funded the eighteen months of high life enjoyed by Beatie, her mother and uncle. It was a dangerous moment, and would have been more dangerous still had Uncle Fitz been present. As it was, Charles was able to imply that the £3000 he loaned to Mr Sumner may have been used for purposes other than that of paying debts. Ince did not give up, but accused Charles of selling horses to Lord Rocksavage and of adding to the price an amount which was then passed on to Beatie. Charles denied this, and Ince did not pursue the point.

A sad moment in the proceedings occurred when the Marchioness of Cholmondeley, formerly Lady Rocksavage, entered the witness box. The grand titles weighed heavily on this spirited young woman of high intelligence, and great good humour. Until that moment, it had all been a great lark for her, an exciting diversion for someone whose social condition provided few outlets for her capabilities. When the case was over, a London correspondent was moved to write to the *Gloucestershire Chronicle*:

In exculpation of the conduct of Lady Cholmondeley, which has filled everybody with surprise, one fact should be stated – at the time when she acted so imprudently she was only 17 years of age. Engaged at 16, and married at 17, with apparently no experience of life and still a mere girl, she probably acted in mere thoughtlessness, and with no such intention as has been attributed to her in quarters where a kindlier judgement would have been accorded her had her age been known.

The first day's proceedings ended with the Court hearing how Fitz Kingscote had accompanied Beatie, her mother and her Uncle Edgar on the trip to Rome in 1882.

When the case was resumed the following day, Mr Davey was still in the business of limiting the damage to his client, Charles Hoare, since much of the evidence heard by then was so damning, particularly that concerning events after Beatie had come of age. He was at pains to tell the Court what it already knew, that the effect of the order making Beatie a ward of court ceased when she came of age, and that the Court 'could not make an order restraining two adult persons from holding communication with each other'. He turned next to the subject of the letters sent by Beatie to Charles, a subject vital to the case, since it was the strongest evidence there was that they had disobeyed the injunction served on each of them – that they should not communicate in any way whatsoever while one of them was in the eyes of the law an infant. That one party, the lady in the case, had despatched letters, and that the other had received them, was indisputable. Davey's defence – a stratagem planned, as we have seen, some time before – was that the recipient did not know from whom they came since the sender's handwriting did not appear on the envelope.

MR JUSTICE CHITTY: If Mr Hoare had sent the letters to the father or to the Court he would have relieved himself of responsibility. That is the strict rule.

MR DAVEY: Mr Hoare would have not had the feeling of a man if he had sent the letters to the Court. Some men would rather die than do such a thing.

MR JUSTICE CHITTY: Some men would sooner die than keep the law, no doubt. But in all this Mr Hoare's mature age and the fact that he was a married man was to be remembered.

From letters, Davey quickly turned to affidavits, particularly that from Major Fitz Kingscote. The chief evidence against Mr Hoare, he argued, was contained in this affidavit from a witness whom, of all others, it would have been expedient to have examined. Once again he asked His Lordship to attach no weight to his evidence except insofar as it was corroborated. What Davey forebore to mention was that Fitz in court would have been harder to discredit than the piece of paper he sent in his stead.

There were a few more exchanges before Mr Justice Chitty delivered his judgement, the most telling of which came from Mr Ince when he described Beatie as 'having suffered a fall from which no woman could live to recover'. Like everybody else present, except Charles, he underrated the lady.

The committal proceedings in this Court of the Chancery Division were highly peculiar. They were not criminal proceedings, but public civil proceedings to enforce a penal process against a public offender. There was no jury, and the judge would decide both fact and law – that is, what had taken place, and what decision should be handed down on the strength of this. He would answer, in effect, yea or nay to 'the motion on behalf of Colonel Kingscote for the committal to prison of Charles Arthur Richard Hoare for contempt in having disobeyed an injunction of the Court'.

Mr Justice Chitty delivered his judgement with a long preamble which summarised in brilliant detail the entire proceedings.[9] Then one by one he spelled out the points at which the people before him were 'found to be in breach of the Court order'. They were left in no doubt that he was in a position to commit them. 'Lady Cholmondeley,' he said, 'undoubtedly committed a breach of the order, and ladies must know, in whatever situation of life they may be, that orders of the Court are not mere pieces of paper binding men only, but that they bind ladies equally.'

However, all was not yet lost. Several things saved Charles from a prison sentence, and those who stood fearfully in his shadow awaiting the outcome. The first was the absence of Major Fitzhardinge Kingscote. The second was the latter's affidavit, which was so revealing in its account of Beatie's behaviour that, as Justice Chitty chose to put it, 'one could not take the word of a man who would so dishonour his own niece'. This was an unkind cut, since the major had merely put in writing the truths that would have been extracted from him in Court. The items of evidence which served most in keeping Charles from prison, however, were those which told of his efforts to obey the court order in the face of temptations to do otherwise, notably on the day Beatie was brought to his hotel with presents she had bought for him in Germany.

The case was closed with the following words from the bench: 'Putting all the circumstances together I think, although I can make an order to commit him [Charles Hoare] I shall do sufficient justice in this case if I order him, as I can do, to pay the costs.'[9]

The newspapers of the day reported the case in great detail. To the modern reader, they seem – rather like accounts of the Wilde trial – remarkably decorous. There was no attempt to get dramatic mileage out of the appearance in Court of so many highly-placed men and women, with all their titles and powerful connections, no descriptions, in the absence of photographs, of their attire, nothing about the way in which they conducted themselves. The weekly papers *Truth* and *Vanity Fair* did, however, have some sharp things to say about what had taken place. In the edition of *Truth* dated 26 March 1885, the editor wrote:

I cannot conceive in whose interest the suit against Mr Hoare was brought. The evil had already been done, and it assuredly was not remedied by washing dirty linen in public. Was Miss Sumner the gainer, or did her parents and relatives who improved the occasion by borrowing money of Mr Hoare profit by this public exposure?[10]

The editor of *Vanity Fair* castigated Colonel Kingscote for taking so long to bring his case to Court, and went on to say that

His grounds, as it turns out, were wholly insufficient, and even had they been sufficient it seems very ill judged on his part to have made an attempt necessarily involving sad disclosures relative to his own family, without the possibility of doing any good whatever, either to them or to the young lady.[11]

Neither *Truth* nor *Vanity Fair*, nor in fact any of the papers, remarked on the strength of feeling that lay behind this extraordinary business. Nobody noted that the Colonel, in his determination to bring Charles Hoare to account for his behaviour, had put at risk his own daughter, the Marchioness of Cholmondeley. This reflected the outrage felt in Gloucestershire by a group of people who had watched in disbelief as a man, ostensibly of their own social class, had flouted the code they held most dear. They were, they might have argued, the party that espoused

> . . . high thought, and amiable words
> And courtliness, and the desire of fame,
> And love of truth, and all that makes a man

– qualities which Charles had, in their eyes, treated with contempt.

If they had hoped – and it was a reasonable hope given the amount of dirty linen exposed to public view – that the cause of all their troubles would now quietly withdraw from the scene, they were mistaken. Charles returned to the attack in Gloucestershire, and the storm continued. Beatie went with him. She probably had no choice; the great houses where she had once been a welcome guest were now closed to her. Her parents, brutally shamed by the whole business, fled the country. They went to Malta, never to return. Arthur Sumner died there in 1895, and his wife moved to Switzerland, where she survived him a further twelve years. Margaret Hoare was now totally alienated from her husband, and the legacy of suffering and bitterness was to affect her family and their descendants well into the twentieth century. Cheerful, bluff, amiable Uncle Fitz, who had strayed into the affair with the first invitation to travel in Europe, and had become so deeply enmeshed that he had to write the pitiful letter to Inderwick in order to disentangle himself, had his marriage brought almost to the point of destruction. Only the compassion and understanding of his gentle Canadian wife, whom her husband's aristocratic relatives despised as a 'colonial', saved it from ruin.

So great was the mayhem in the wake of the 'Gloucestershire Scandal', as it came to be called in the newspapers, that even the philanthropic gesture which Charles made in apparent expiation for what he had done – founding the *Mercury* – seemed empty. The cynical saw it as a cover for his continued relationship with Beatie, who could appear at the school as a housekeeper or matron.

In his judgement Mr Justice Chitty had remarked on 'the cumbersome manner in which Mr Hoare gave his evidence'. It was the only aside in all that was said and written about the case which revealed something of the bearing of the man at the centre of it. Cumbersome was an understatement: he was crushingly insensitive, bullying those people he could not buy. It was evident that he had reached mature years without reaching maturity. Neither the fields of Devon nor the 'university of the world' had brought him the disciplines which lead to freedom and the ability to choose sensibly among the many alternatives that life offers. A lifetime of self-indulgence, fuelled by his enormous income from the family banking business, had left him without the strategies to cope with a girl of fire and character. He must, however, have begun to realise that in Beatie Sumner he had stumbled on an original, a one-off.

They left the court together, Charles with his meagre absolution and lighter in pocket by hundreds of pounds in legal fees. Later that year he would found his new school, the *Mercury*, not knowing that it was to become his refuge, the source of his transformation into a totally different kind of man, and the basis of an astonishing career for his mistress.

6 – Binstead Hard

After the court case Charles wasted time, money and effort that could have gone into setting up the *Mercury*. He fought tenaciously to retain some elements of the only way of life he knew. The fight began in Cirencester.

In April a meeting of subscribers, members and owners of coverts in the V.W.H. Hunt was held at The King's Head Hotel, convened, as it was delicately put, 'by circular issued by the Hunt Secretary, Mr Edward Trinder, rendered necessary by the serious differences of opinion existing on the question of the retention of the Mastership by Mr C. A. R. Hoare.'[1]

About a hundred men gathered in one of the public rooms of the hotel, those supporting Charles slightly outnumbering those against him. Earl Bathurst was in the chair, and at his side were the Earl of Suffolk and Berkshire, Sir Michael Hicks-Beach MP, and Mr W. Cripps. Nearby were other landowners, some of them the ancestors of people who would own and farm the same land nearly a century later.

To Lord Bathurst fell the duty of spelling out the business of the meeting, put more bluntly this time: the demand for the resignation of Charles Hoare as Master of the V.W.H. He spoke of years of 'unpleasant gossip and unpleasant reports pervading the country'. On mentioning the man at the centre of it, he added, 'I observe he is present, and therefore anything I say of course he can contradict.'

It was a long speech, suggesting the dismay of a man, for long comfortable in his wealth and power, who felt unexpectedly threatened. The listeners heard how Charles, who was in any case no longer on speaking terms with Lord Bathurst, had sent a letter to another member of the hunt, who had shunned him in similar fashion, saying he would take the hounds back to kennels if that member appeared in the field again. Charles had sent a copy of the letter to Lord Bathurst, but then, as the Earl drily put it, 'kindly made an exception in my case'. Referring to the trial and his presence there, he went on, 'I was not called on, but I confess it was with considerable surprise that I heard facts admitted which I had been solemnly assured were absolutely false.'

When Lord Suffolk spoke it was to remind the company that a year previously people had signed a petition, or 'memorial', asking that Charles be allowed to continue as Master. He told how, just as the deputation was about to leave the room, one of them had said he would like to know what Charles had done. Now they all knew, and the man had to go.

There were more speeches in the same vein, Sir Michael following Lord Suffolk, then Mr Cripps. All of them attacked Charles; but soon others would have their say, and their cue came from a man who professed his neutrality, saying that he came before them as a stranger, but one who had been devoted to fox-hunting all his life. Reginald Herbert had spent his honeymoon at Kelsey, 'the charming and picturesque seat of Mr C. A. R. Hoare', and he implied what the majority were waiting to hear – that a new Master would not be allowed to ride over the country, so strong was the feeling on 'the other side', meaning the tenant farmers. There were loud cheers at this, and cries of 'Hear, hear'. Gradually the farmers gained confidence and spoke up for Charles.

One did, however, have the temerity to speak against him. Charles was immediately on his feet, launching into a speech that was as bullying as that at the Hunt Puppy Show had been sycophantic. 'Let them have it!' shouted a supporter as he got into his stride. He catalogued all he had done for the country, and was cheered all the way. Referring to the scandal he said, 'It seems that but for this moral technicality you would have nothing to say against me.'

He sat down to applause, and remained quiet while the meeting discussed the possibility of canvassing the membership to see if the same support would be found for his continuance in office as in the previous year. Mr Flux, a landowner, brought the company back to the scandal again.

'It has been published everywhere,' Flux said. 'It is in the face of the world that the gentleman in question himself went into the witness box and was examined by his own counsel – the ablest men of the day – and that no one is able to clear that gentleman of one particle of the soil with which he dirtied himself in the witness box.'

Flux went on: 'He admitted it – the father of a family which lives before us Cirencester people had to admit himself the father of another child by a young lady, whose name need not be mentioned, with whom he was living. He admitted the occasion for the injunction and that as long as the injunction prevailed and there was peril –'

Charles exploded.

'The meeting has nothing to do with this!'

His men roared their support. When the cheering stopped, Flux lamely tried to resume his speech, but was shouted down. There were a few more speeches before the meeting broke up, including one from a farmer who tried vainly to bring the opposing factions together. But there was to be no reconciliation that evening, and the meeting ended with nothing resolved beyond a decision to canvas the whole membership to see if Charles had as many supporters as before. When this was done a few weeks later, and it was found that he had enough people on his side to make it possible, he split the hunt, setting up his own quarters in Cricklade, eight miles from Swindon on the road to Cirencester, so that by the following year there were two V.W.H. Hunt clubs, the Cricklade under Charles Hoare and the Cirencester under Lord Bathurst.

The division was to last for over eighty years, by which time enough generations of huntsmen and women had come and gone for the whole unruly business to have been forgotten, and the membership united again.

The summer of 1885 was spent finding a sailing ship to use as a nautical school. When, in later years, people asked among themselves why Charles began this enterprise there were no firm answers to be had. There was, of course, the precedent of his yacht at Exmouth being used to train boys for the sea during the time he lived at Luscombe Castle: while some saw the school as a gesture designed to alleviate some of the opprobrium that followed in the wake of the trial, others believed that the decision to start a school stemmed from a recognition of the needs of the woman with whom Charles was now allied. Though refusing a divorce, Margaret Hoare had left him, taking his sons and their daughter Agatha with her. In her place he had a woman of enormous energy – even in her eighties she could work a sixteen-hour day – for which he had to provide an outlet. The hunting fields of Gloucestershire, and probably of the whole British Isles, were now barred to her. The ship would give her an outdoor life and things to do, but it must have seemed a forlorn hope that she would adapt to a world so different from that she had known.

In the London docks Charles found the barque *Illovo*, named after a river in South Africa. He bought her and re-christened her *Mercury*. She had been built in Aberdeen by H. Hall & Company for Thomas Rennie and her first master, Alexander Airth. She was quite small, approximately 400 gross tons, only 139 feet long, with a width – her 'beam' in nautical language – of 27 feet. She had begun life as a ship-rigged vessel, but her rig had been changed and by 1880 she was recorded in Lloyd's list as a barque. By comparison the *Cutty Sark*, perhaps the most famous merchant sailing ship ever built, is 963 gross tons, with an overall length of 280 feet and a beam of 36 feet. The small dimensions of the *Illovo* had enabled her to cross the

sand bars on the African coast and to trade with places inaccessible
to most sea-going ships of the time.

Charles converted the ship into a replica of an early nineteenth-
century warship. The hatches were removed and replaced with
gratings that let in light and air to the 'tween deck immediately
below. The 'tween deck was fitted out with tables and mess fittings so
like those of a man-o'-war that one half expected to see a cannon in
between each table, in the manner of HMS *Victory*. Weather-proofed
stowage was provided on the main deck for hammocks, again in the
style of a fighting ship under sail, where the sailors' bedding gave
them protection from enemy gunfire. Mooring booms hung from the
sides – long timbers, like sections of masts, which could be swung
out at right angles to the ship, reaching out over the water to provide
access in all weathers.

Not content with all this, Charles bought the topsail schooner
Diana, 41 tons, as a tender to the ship, and in summer months
twenty-five boys at a time used the schooner for cruises in the
Channel. He bought small boats for instruction in sailing and
rowing, and even a steam launch, in which boys learned the
rudiments of engineering.

A staff of fifteen was recruited to administer the ship and instruct
the boys, made up of two ex-naval officers and thirteen able-seaman
pensioners. With them came the first intake of boys. They were said
to be 'improved street arabs of fourteen or fifteen years of age who
have vouched for themselves that they are willing to enter the Royal
Navy', picked up from the slums of London and quarantined at a
cottage in Tooting before being sent to the ship. There, as an Isle of
Wight paper put it, they would be 'saved from temporal and eternal
ruin'.[2]

The site for the training ship, or 'nautical school', was chosen with
care. The old village of Binstead is a little to the west of Ryde in the
Isle of Wight, between the main road and the Solent. Most visitors to
the island fail to notice it: a lane leads into the village and back out

71

again, the village has no obvious attractions, and the beaches on that side of the island are uninteresting and almost inaccessible. Charles and Beatie moved into a large house standing between the shore line to the north and the old village church, which together with a screen of trees hid it from prying eyes. They anchored the *Mercury* just offshore of the house, where she would be afloat at all stages of the tide. There was a ready-made causeway – Binstead Hard – reaching out to the ship. Put there by the Normans, it had served to carry Quarr stone out to the boats which shipped it away to construct old Southampton, Winchester Cathedral, and even parts of Dover Castle and the Tower of London. Now it would be a humble ingredient in another, if smaller, chapter in English history.

Their preparations made, the lovers began a seven-year exile, cut off from the outside world, but near enough to be able to obtain provisions for themselves and their new community.

Since neither Beatie nor Charles had ever been to school they could bring to the running of the *Mercury* a style all their own. It was to be unlike any other school in the country – the traditional boarding schools, the reformatories, or any of the residential schools then prevailing, let alone the board schools, with their rows of desks and pupils learning their tables and capes and bays by rote. The staff of instructors knew what skills to impart to their pupils, what would give them an advantage when they joined the training establishments of the Royal Navy or the crew of a rich man's yacht. They might have had strong views on how this should be done, but if they thought they were going to re-create on the *Mercury* the rigours of life on, say, a warship, they were much mistaken, even though the ship had been converted to look like one. Discipline in these early years was going to come not from the threat of punishment, but from example – and Beatie herself was to provide the example.

She set about mastering all the skills of a sailor, bringing to them the same zeal and energy that she had addressed to the business of riding. She took to wearing male attire so that she could go aloft, up the ratlines and along the footropes of the highest yards, eighty feet or more above the deck, and she did it in bare feet, winter and summer, as she expected the boys to do. She trimmed her hair to reduce her femininity, so that people would see her less as a woman striving in a man's world, and more as someone who could succeed across any range of activities open to someone young, fit and intelligent. She ignored changing fashions, for to have changed with them would have been to depart from the course she had set herself, consistent in everything she did once she had set her mind to a task, whether it took days or decades to complete. She could row a boat as well as any man – she was still rowing in her seventies – and ferried herself out to the ship every morning to be on deck before the boys got up at six. Their first exercise of the morning – as described by an old *Mercury* boy who died many years ago – was to go aloft, regardless of the weather, 'over the port rigging, at the top by the futtock shrouds, avoiding lubbers' hole, and down by the starboard side'. No instructor needed to flourish a cane or a rope's end to drive them on: they reacted in response to Beatie's leadership. The boys swam in the Solent every day, beginning at Easter regardless of when it fell in the calendar and continuing right through to October, and she swam with them. She learned to sail a boat, and forty years later she was still taking boys out on the Hamble in whalers, teaching them the niceties of tacking, gybing and running before the wind.

As the cycle of training was repeated again and again over the years, Beatie grew more competent than her own staff. She lacked their practical experience of long voyages, being limited to the occasional short cruise on the *Diana*, but on the *Mercury* itself, at its anchorage off Binstead, she was supreme. She soon knew enough to hire and fire men without consulting others, and did so until her death, sixty-one years after she had first set foot on the ship.

Very few people outside the ship knew of Beatie's part in its management; none saw her in action. She had become, and would remain all her life, an exceedingly shy person. When a reporter from the Isle of Wight *Observer*[3] was allowed on board in April 1890, he was shown round by Charles. He found the ship alive with activity. Small boys, newcomers to the ranks, were exercising with dumb-bells in one corner of the main deck, while in another parallel bars had been set up on mats and an instructor was taking older boys through elaborate gymnastics. Lessons in seamanship took place on deck, and the whole ship was their classroom. Below decks was a classroom in which boys learned the '3Rs', working on slates. Around the ship there was a constant traffic of boats, some plying between Binstead and Ryde, fetching stores and water, others with boys rowing and sailing as if in constant preparation for a regatta.

Charles frequently left their island exile to continue his private war with the landowners of Gloucestershire. He attacked them in letters to the county papers written from Boodles, deriding the efforts of Lord Bathurst to stay in the hunting field with the old V.W.H. The land he had rented, ostensibly for the shooting, now came to the fore in his plan to frustrate the people opposed to him. When boundaries were at last drawn between the territories of the old and the new V.W.H., some of the landowners found themselves trapped inside the latter and unable to ride across country without permission from the man with whom they were in conflict.

For longer and longer spells Beatie was left in charge of the ship. In the absence of Charles her competence grew: the young woman, still only in her twenties, was setting a style for herself, and for those around her, which would take them through almost to the middle of the next century.

Two events brought Charles down to earth and back to the ship for good. Having won, as he thought, a victory over the landowners on the matter of territorial boundaries, he decided to examine the treasurer's records for the previous five years, and calculated that he was owed £3250 in unpaid hunt subscriptions. When the money was not forthcoming he prepared to pursue the matter in the courts.

Battle lines were drawn, and Earls Bathurst and Suffolk agreed to engage Sir Henry James, who had been Arthur Sumner's counsel in the Court of Chancery, to act for them. (Lord Suffolk, writing to his fellow Earl, said, 'I suspect he would prefer to act for a couple of dukes, but perhaps he will settle for a brace of earls'[3].) With their solicitors they composed statements which would constitute their defence; inevitably there was reference to the scandal and to the case that had been heard in court in March 1885. Charles was furious. To him it was a trick on the part of the earls to deny him payment of subscriptions. All the details of what had happened between him and Beatie would be paraded again, just as he was beginning to hope that the past was over and done with and a new life starting for his second family. His solicitors appealed on his behalf for the relevant paragraph to be withdrawn, or, as they saw it, 'to have the action fought on fair grounds'.[4]

By now it was the spring of 1888. Two years of independence with his own pack in what was in effect his own country had brought Charles no real pleasure nor any perceptible gain. In June Lord Bathurst wrote to Lord Suffolk to say, 'I wish carefully to guard myself from any imputation of over-confidence that the inscrutable Mr Hoare will drop his action against us, but I think it is probable that his solicitor's appeal . . . was a parting shot on the off-chance of our giving way.'[5] Lord Suffolk, equally cautious, replied that 'I cordially and entirely agree with you. Never Holloa till you are some distance out of a Hoare wood . . .'[6] In the event, Charles not only dropped the case but left the county. He loaned his hounds to another man and returned to Binstead.[7]

The second event was a blow from another quarter, finally bringing to an end more than a decade of recklessness. The business world was closing ranks. He was asked to relinquish his post as senior partner in the Hoare Bank. The only surprise was that the request had taken so long in coming. On the company's books were the accounts of families related to those whom he had most offended. He had dissipated the equivalent of millions of pounds in modern money, and to no very good purpose, unless one sought to elevate the affair with Beatie to a more exalted plane. He was not, however, left destitute. As a senior partner in the bank he could dictate his own terms, and these were enviable: half the profits of the bank for life, and the same to be paid into his estate for a further seven years after his death. The figures involved are said to have been in the region of £40,000 a year, in excess of £1 million a year in modern money.

In the isolation of Binstead the lovers began to change. Paradoxically, it took the form of a softening of the one and a hardening of the other. The arrogant Charles was to soften into the figure whom C. B. Fry would later describe as possessing 'a genius for kindness', whereas Beatie was to harden into the grim, intense woman who left her mark on the minds and bodies (literally as well as figuratively) of thousands of boys who came into her charge.

For a decade some of these boys and a handful of ex-naval men were to be their only constant company. Charles was to enter on a work of love which would survive him and prove a source of enchantment for as long as there were people to admire artistry and craftsmanship. Beatie, whom one suspects had encouraged the excesses which had brought misfortune to so many, was to find an outlet for the tremendous will she had to shape the lives of others. The *Mercury* was to prove too small a stage for her incredible powers. She was Sarah Bernhardt playing a village hall, a Boadicea relegated to minor skirmishes.

7 – The Good Ship

The most striking innovation in the new school began innocently enough, yet it brought it into the mainstream of normal life and perhaps set educational precedents.

The boys were on hand twenty-four hours a day, week in, week out, and they needed more pastimes than were at first envisaged. In the evenings especially it was hard to find things to do and they would often sing together, much as the huntsmen did in Cirencester when the rain went on too long. The standard of entertainment went up sharply when there arrived among the earlier recruits to the staff a tailor, James McGavin. He was a Scot, and he could play the accordion and the tin whistle. Impromptu sing-songs turned to formal concerts on the orlop deck, with staff and boys rehearsing their 'party pieces' under his tutelage. Charles and Beatie came on board to attend these concerts and were sufficiently impressed to persuade McGavin to give up tailoring for music. It was one of those rare instances of a remarkable talent receiving the patronage it deserved. McGavin was allowed to buy band instruments and music, at first to teach himself, and then the boys. He was so successful that the ship was barely three years into its history before it was necessary to build a recreation hall ashore so that this new dimension to their lives could have the setting it deserved. Every boy was given a chance to learn to play a brass, woodwind or percussion instrument. In time string instruments were added, and these would play separately in what McGavin chose to call the 'string band'. The impact on the life of the ship was considerable. The boys proved apt pupils and were soon competent enough to play on bandstands all over the Isle of Wight.

Those who could not master an instrument were encouraged to sing in a choir, and the few who could neither play nor sing were taught to dance, so that eventually the whole ship's company, over 130 boys, was caught up in music making. Bugles were introduced into the routine and the day began with 'reveille' and ended with the 'Last Post' – that tune of haunting simplicity, a valediction to the day, carrying across the water to the house where Charles, Beatie and the little Sybil gathered round an open window to hear it. Prayers were said morning and evening on the ship, and hymns were introduced. In the evening the boys sang to the house so that its inhabitants would feel that they were taking part in their worship.

The most notable effect of the new musical life was Beatie. The tours of Europe with her mother and Uncle Fitz had been unremarkable, travels of the kind that people undertook for perhaps no better reason than to keep up with their peers, to have something to talk about at social gatherings. Now new realms of pleasure were opened to her as McGavin coaxed better and better music from the boys. She would have liked to visit London to hear great orchestras play, but she could not face the risk of encountering people who remembered all too well the events of March 1885, and all that had gone before. But if she could not go to London she would go to the Continent, to Bayreuth. McGavin had opened her ears to Mozart and Beethoven, but above all to Wagner. The huge portentous drama of *The Ring* cycle complemented something in the inner life of the passionate young woman. In time, one of Wagner's operas was to transform her life and that of her lover.

So much was happening on the ship that Charles began the *Training Ship Mercury Magazine* in 1889, with the opening edition covering that and the previous four years.[1] It was printed to a high standard and was for sale outside the ship, the editor advertising that 'subscribers of one shilling and sixpence a year will be entitled to a copy being forwarded to them Post Free every month.' It could hardly be described as compulsive reading, consisting for the most part of a rag-bag of ship's activities, schoolboy jokes and stirring adventure stories in which gallant British sailors overcame colonial mountebanks, weathered terrible storms, and defended a roseate Kipling-haunted Empire. Pages of hilarious profundities went *bras dessous* with doggerel written by the boys. One such poem began:

> I am a Dover lad!
> A happy card am I
> I stand upon the beach
> I watch the sea birds fly.
>
> I hear great fame about a ship
> That ship I want to see,
> So now I'm off to the Isle of Wight
> To join the 'Mercury'.

There were details of 'entertainments' held in the Recreation Hall, such as 'A short extravaganza written and arranged by C. L. Mackay, in which he will recite the Dagger and Ghost scene from "Macbeth" ', followed by 'McLean's Musical, Whimsical, and Eccentrical Absurdities; including a Parody on the celebrated Song "Who's that a-calling so sweet" '.

No matter how awful the contents of the earlier editions of the magazine, the delight that Charles took in his latest venture, the care, education and training of boys from the humblest imaginable beginnings, was apparent throughout. The former Master of Fox Hounds was now content to play third man in a cricket match between his boys and 'a team of gentlemen representing the Isle of Wight College' . . . 'Mr C. A. R. Hoare *c.* Whittall, *b.* Whittall, 6' – a far cry from the matches in Cirencester Park with Lord Bathurst. The man who had stunned Gloucestershire society with his extravagance and insensitivity watched over his boys with something that resembled tenderness and affection. They were driven hard by the instructors he employed, but there was no brutality. In a contemporary account of one of the 'entertainments' Charles is described as entering the recreation hall to be greeted from right and left by the boys in the audience, all totally unafraid of him, unawed, and hugely enjoying his companionship. They owed him everything – the clothes they wore, the food on their tables, the hammocks they slept in at night – but such was his relationship with them that they felt no sense of condescension on his part, and were grateful without having to grovel.

Beatie's part in the life of the ship was never directly referred to in the magazine. But on leaving boys would address their letters of gratitude to her as often as to Charles, and these were printed. In March 1890 a boy who had gone on to the Royal Navy wrote from HMS *Impregnable* in Devonport:

Dear Madam,

I now take the pleasure of writing these few lines hoping to find you quite well, and to thank you for the kindness of writing to us boys.

I am pleased to hear the ship is getting on so well. I am a Petty Officer boy, and I get on well with my instructions, and I thank Mr Hoare for the instructions received while I was on the *Mercury*, and I wish I had learnt more than I did. I shall be a first class boy in two weeks' time.

I should very much like a likeness of the racing crews when we had it taken in France, and one of the Ship, if you would be so kind as to send me one; for it brings back remembrance of old times when we was there.

Dear Madam, you must forgive me for not writing before. We all send our respects to you and Mr Hoare and we shall always be glad to hear the Ship highly spoken of. I must conclude.

I remain, Yours obediently,
S. Cobbledick.

The reference to France in young Cobbledick's letter arose out of the only long voyage made by the ship in her role as a training ship. When Charles finally had to leave Gloucestershire in 1888 he determined to prove that the *Mercury* was no mere showpiece. In October he prepared her for sea, but said nothing to the boys until the day came to hoist anchor. Neither Charles nor Beatie went on the voyage for reasons that remain obscure. The only accounts of what followed are those of the boys themselves, telling in simple language what happened between the first attempt to get out of harbour and their return in April of the following year.

Willis, No. 171, describes the first day, 19 October:

The same day as we got under way, we were at dinner, when the Chief Officer, Henderson, came and ordered silence which was immediately obeyed and he said that we was to get under way this afternoon, as soon as Mr Hoare came aboard to say goodbye to us. At the joyful news, we all gave three cheers, which made the ship ring from stem to stern. The chief officer said we would all be sick before night, which I am sorry to say we were.

There was a lot of letter writing to do, to be ready to give to Mr Hoare, when he came aboard to post for us, and then we began to be restless waiting. About three o'clock Mr Hoare and Mr Marshall, the secretary, came on board with some marbles for us to play with at Gibraltar. Mr Hoare spoke very kindly to us, and pardoned every boy for his conduct, so as he should have as much chance as any other boy. We had six marbles and a glassy each, and with a parting cheer from the rigging, which we had manned, the noble T.S.M. hove out of sight, round the point off Cowes, and in a very short time we were flying past the Needles.

A senior boy, John Blackwell, 'Captain of the 1st Division', says that the band was on the poop, 'and struck the tune "Goodbye Sweetheart"'. He adds that there were 132 boys on the ship and 20 seamen.

Once the voyage had started, there was little or no discussion with the boys on their whereabouts. After eleven days under sail Blackwell writes, 'we turned out at the usual time [and] we were astonished to find ourselves sailing round the Isle of Wight.' The ship was taking in water through a faulty valve, and repairs were completed in Portsmouth, with the ship ready to sail on 13 November. They were towed out of harbour and made plain sail, only to find that the rudder was faulty.

It was 1 December before they finally got away, but even this attempt was nearly thwarted when they had to shelter for five days off

St Helens, on the east coast of the Isle of Wight, waiting for a storm to abate.

There was a desperate quality about the venture from then on. They fought their way down the Channel and into the Bay of Biscay. The ship was overcrowded, and at times life on deck was so dangerous that the men in charge ordered the boys below, where they stayed for days at a time. They spent Christmas day in Gibraltar, and by New Year's Day were in the Golfe du Lion riding out a storm which lasted six days, with the boys confined to their hammocks. The professional sailors had to tie themselves to the masts so that they would not be swept overboard by the huge seas thundering aft along the decks.

They stayed at Villefranche for two months and then started for home in good sailing weather, stopping only to pick up stores and water at Gibraltar on 28 March. The week before Easter 1889 found them coming up the Channel, and they anchored off Binstead on Easter Sunday.

In the absence of concrete evidence, one can only speculate about why Charles and Beatie insisted on the voyage going ahead in the dead of winter. Sail training, on ships that actually undertook long voyages, was notoriously dangerous. In 1880 HMS *Atalanta* left Bermuda with a crew of 280, most of them boys in their teens, on a training cruise. She was never seen again. In March 1878, HMS *Eurydice* sank off the Isle of Wight; only two of a crew of 350 were saved. Among the dead was Lieutenant the Hon. Edward Robert Gifford, second son of Lord Gifford by the Hon. Frederica Fitzhardinge Berkeley, the eldest daughter of Admiral Lord Berkeley. The Admiral was the first Baron, married to the daughter of the Duke of Richmond, and Beatie's great-uncle. Beatie may well have attended Gifford's funeral, and so knew only too well the risk involved in putting the *Mercury* to sea. Charles, with his present of marbles and a pardon for every boy, knew it too. If they were hoping to impress people with the viability of their venture in the wake of humiliation in Gloucestershire and in the banking world, they were doing so at appalling risk to the lives of others. Why did they not go on the voyage themselves? Had the whole idea of the school begun to weigh too heavily on people whose lives had hitherto been taken up in a colourful social round? Was their relationship wearing thin, with the need for a release from responsibilities to solve personal problems?

A second child, Keith Robin, was born to Charles and Beatie on 26 September 1890. Quite how they explained away this aspect of their lives in the eyes of society must remain a matter of speculation: one can only assume that, in the comparative isolation of Binstead, they passed themselves off as a normal family. A clue to this lay in the practice of calling Beatie 'Madame' in her own home, at least from the middle of the Binstead period. This became so ingrained that in time even her own family used this form of address; and C. B. Fry, when he married her, used the word as a name rather than as a title, introducing her to people with 'This is my Madame', and calling her 'Madame' even in their private life.

If it served to distance Beatie from the people outside her household, it cannot have lent itself to an easy and affectionate relationship within.

Charles moved his entire establishment to Hamble in the spring of 1892. Seven years of isolation had cooled the passions roused by the 'Gloucestershire Scandal', and they could contemplate an end to their self-imposed exile. Hamble was a more practical site for a number of reasons. Charles still had a business life to pursue, with properties in London and the provinces to control, which he could get to with greater ease if he lived on the mainland. And if privacy was important, Hamble, then an obscure little village well away from the main road, provided it. The *Mercury* suffered the same problems as those that beset *Britannia*, the forerunner of the Royal Naval College, Dartmouth. *Britannia* had been anchored at Portland in 1862, but in severe weather the boys could be marooned on the ship for days at a time. Within eighteen months the ship was moved to Dartmouth, which offered not only shelter but room for the development of a shore establishment. The anchorage at Hamble provided the same benefits for the *Mercury*, which was exposed to the full force of easterly gales at Binstead. The move to the river enabled Charles to lay out playing fields, and to put up permanent buildings, classrooms and a recreation hall – important factors, considering the limited life span of a sailing ship.

At Hamble the ship was anchored mid-river, her bows directed upstream. Work began on a twenty-five-room mansion which Charles had designed himself. It was the sort of house he had been accustomed to all his life, with rooms set aside for every kind of activity. It was a strange potpourri of architectural styles, no doubt culled from the many houses he had owned or rented over nearly thirty years. To the trained architect it was not a success; its obtruding features showed little sense of balance or symmetry, and some of the windows were badly proportioned. Charles may not have been all that pleased with it himself, as he sent a photograph of the house to Lady Hoare at Stourhead House in Wiltshire on the back of which he wrote 'The Institution'.

The main block of the house was four storeys high with a two-storey wing, the lower floor of which contained store rooms, a workroom where boys' clothes were ironed and repaired, and a laundry, while the upper housed a rapidly growing collection of naval artefacts and was in effect a private museum, becoming in time one of the best of its kind in the world. There were models of ships, yachts, paddle steamers and boats of every description, together with models of typical naval paraphernalia, such as 'Captain Beadon's torpedo-shaped buoy', 'Mr Hookey's invention for bending planks', and 'Commander Westbrook's standard Tide gauge'.

In the right angle made by the main block and the two-storey wing was built a conservatory which came to be called the 'Verandah', and was used occasionally as a classroom. The space outside, which in later years was to become the parade ground where inspections took place, was surrounded by rustic poles and trellises supporting roses and climbing plants.

Now that she was living on the mainland and was closer to the traffic of people, Beatie was more cautious about displaying her athleticism. She was much less active on the sailing ship; her exploits in the rigging and her swims with the boys came to an end, but she still sailed on the river and rowed herself out to the ship. Her manly garb was confined to a floppy bow tie on what looked very much like a man's shirt, but she retained the short hair style she had adopted on arriving at Binstead.

By 1896 there was a thriving community ashore and afloat. Lloyd's Yacht Register for that year shows that 'Captain Hoare' had four yachts – the *Mercury*, *Pantomime* (153 tons), *Thalia* (13 tons), and *Whisper* (17 tons). All were in constant use: the *Mercury* was at permanent anchor and was where the boys slept, dined and did most of their training, while the others served as tenders, taking them on short cruises into the Solent and beyond.

In 1897 Charles and Beatie went to Bayreuth to attend a performance of Wagner's *Parsifal*. Beatie was deeply moved. She protested that it was the music which affected her, but it requires no great leap of the imagination to assume that it was the story as much as its musical setting which stirred her. She could easily identify with Kundry, the witch-like woman in the opera, who inhabited a world of knights and castles, much as the young Beatie had lived among the aristocrats of Gloucestershire in their castle and country houses. Like Kundry, she was an achiever, and, like Kundry, she had been the downfall of men.

Charles, for his part, had more than a touch of Parsifal. Ignorant of the world, shut off from reality, first as a boy in Luscombe Castle, and then behind the barricade of money that came soon after, he could be seen as the 'innocent fool' of the story who would attain to a purposeful life only through pain and suffering.

Like Kundry and Parsifal, Beatie and Charles found redemption and peace in the rituals of the Christian church. They became intensely religious after their return from Bayreuth, and their relationship from then on was on a different footing. They contemplated in a new light the enormity of their conduct, of lives damaged by their affair, the relatives in exile and others humiliated by the prurient interest of people in those who had been involved in what was, by Victorian standards, a monumental scandal. Margaret Hoare's every appearance in the hunting field was the signal for crowds to gather for the vicarious thrill of looking at her, a victim in the story. But the former lovers could not undo the damage they had done.

They began their new relationship by living in separate houses, with Charles moving into Hall Place, West Meon, twenty miles from Hamble. Then they tried to make the *Mercury* a religious establishment rather than a mere training ship for boys. In Beatie's hands it was not a happy endeavour, but happiness in any normal sense of the word was not her objective. Redemption through suffering was to become the keynote of her religion. The material comforts of her life were considerable, but she drove herself as hard as she drove the people around her. Life, as she was later to tell parents, was a struggle from birth to Home, a struggle she willingly accepted. She grew in time to merit Lord Rosebery's arresting description of Cromwell as 'a practical mystic, the most formidable and terrible of all combinations.'[2]

The first practical result of the visit to Bayreuth was the Building, the name given to the theatre which Beatie built in the grounds overlooking the Hamble. It was unique in several ways, not least because it was probably the only theatre constructed in the nineteenth century at the instigation of a woman and paid for by her. It was designed by Romanes Walker and modelled on Wagner's theatre in Bayreuth. It was, to quote from the programme notes of a play performed there in the 1930s, built in accordance with Wagner's well-known principles, and internally so designed that each member of the audience has a clear uninterrupted view of the stage; and the orchestra, with space for forty performers, is sunk so that the musicians being out of sight the music may be heard and the action on the stage seen without the inevitable distraction caused by a visible orchestra.[3]

It seated over three hundred people, though the seating was rather spartan. The stage measured forty-two feet by twenty-six feet, and was 'fully equipped, being able to deal . . . with the most difficult requirements that an ingenious producer may call for'. It was paid for with money from the sale of some of Beatie's jewellery.

The mystical dimension of Beatie's Bayreuth transformation was expressed in some notes she made at the time. Their clumsiness makes the reader wonder why she ever let them out of her possession:

A hired pen, a restless imaginative mind and two marks of 'Beautiful Parsifal' anyone must put capitals to Parsifal and take off their hats the man who wrote the notes down, the Sounds are Divine and the man heard it from his soul. It teaches you as nothing can if you will but understand it takes you from the depths of yourself and your sordid mean ambitious selfishness and general unrighteousness and puts you with the 'Green Hill King' at rest, among heights of beauty, thoughts of toil from fit to Peace, the Peace which passeth all understanding others familiar to leave it and go out and show you have tested it by acting what you heard and wanted to say. That's Parsifal all fearless, temptations passed, love conquered it always while it always must. When you cannot hear the music when you feel all shaky and queer put what you love best in the floating clouds that are tipped with the end of golden density of sunset as your mood may be. Take them to be your loving instinct show them there and think of all you know best, what good if you knew Parsifal drew out its triumphant lore, notes get at the nature of its triumph when every instrument in the vast orchestra shouts screams will have its note of triumph for good and all nature does the same. All our natures to come through as Parsifal did but for others we can try and when we are tired Richard Wagner. What then? He answered me through it all cannot you understand you can Buck up and try more.[4] (sic)

This garbled attempt to put feelings into words was printed in yet another programme used in the theatre. Luckily for the authoress, perhaps, it was reproduced in her original handwriting, which was so indecipherable that very few people were likely to struggle beyond the first line or two. Even with the addition of a few well-placed commas and full-stops it remains incoherent, and is evidence enough that here was a woman gripped by overwhelming emotions, and crippled by her inability to communicate them to others. Fortunately for her, as for few others, the means were at hand to construct a tangible expression of her feelings – the theatre.

In a calmer moment Beatie composed a dedication for the Building, and had the words carved in stone and mounted on the south wall next to a life-size figure of Christ crucified. It read:

DEDICATED TO MINDS THAT CAN
SOAR, THAT WILL RISE AND NOT
BE DISCOURAGED BY OBSTACLES OR
DIFFICULTIES, THAT WILL CHANCE
AND DARE FOR WHAT THEY LOVE
AND KNOW TO BE RIGHT.

TO CO-OPERATION, COMBINATION,
DASH, PERSEVERANCE, AND
UNSELFISHNESS, THIS T.S. 'MERCURY'
AND ITS ADJUNCTS ARE FEARLESSLY
DEDICATED. FOR HARMONY, THE
GOOD OF MANKIND AND TO HEARTS
THAT CAN BEAT FOR OTHERS.
ITS IDEAL IS GOOD FRIDAY'S HERO.[5]

To all outward appearances the community at Hamble was self-contained, little affected by pressures from the outside world. However, the ship's magazine for 1898 advertised places in the school for those 'able to pay the small premium of £20 per annum, which sum is £10 less than the actual cost of maintaining each boy', a sign that the days of the *Mercury* as a charitable school funded entirely by Charles were over.

Other events were taking place beyond the community which would impinge upon it. Margaret Hoare was living at Kelsey Manor,

Kent, the home of Charles's mother. All round her the fields were being snapped up by property developers as rural Beckenham turned into London suburbia, and she decided to move. She went first to Canada to visit her son Wilfred who was working on a ranch, taking Agatha with her; but when they arrived Wilfred told her that they must return at once to England, and he would go with them. He was shocked by his mother's appearance, convinced that she was a sick woman. On their return it was found that she had cancer. Charles could not have been indifferent to her suffering, as a reconciliation of sorts took place when Wilfred, who had made his own way in life in the absence of parental help and guidance, was invited to help manage the *Mercury*. True reconciliation took place in 1899 when Charles, urged on by his son, at last made peace with the woman from whom he had so long been estranged. She died on 7 October 1899, and was buried in the family mausoleum in Beckenham.

In June the previous year Beatrice Holme Sumner had married the sportsman and journalist Charles Burgess Fry.

8 – *Superman and Superwoman*

C.B. was twenty-six when he married Beatie and ten years her junior. He was the most famous and, in the opinion of many, the most handsome man in England. When the newsboys cried 'Fry wins again!' or 'C.B. scores another century!' people knew at once whose victories were being celebrated. Lord Birkenhead, the 2nd earl, in his biography of his father, described C.B. as 'a Greek god, so beautiful in face and body that he might have been wrought by the chisel of Praxiteles, with broad shoulders and narrow hips'.[1]

C.B. was born in April 1872, the eldest son of Mr and Mrs Lewis Fry, formerly of Rotherfield in Sussex. His earliest memories were of life in a house near the Chislehurst tunnel in Kent, not far from Charles Hoare's house, Kelsey Manor. Mr Fry was a civil engineer who could afford to send his son to preparatory school, but was probably relieved when, in 1885, the boy won a scholarship to Repton, where he was to manifest that outstanding skill in cricket which was to make him world famous.

After six years at Repton C.B. went up to Wadham College, Oxford. The college had a poor reputation in those days, giving rise to the undergraduate riddle 'Why is the Wadham boat like Noah's Ark?' to which the answer was 'Because it moves slowly upon the face of the waters and is filled with all manner of beasts.'[2]

In 1891 the college attracted a new generation of men so brilliant that their time at Wadham came to be regarded as one of intellectual renaissance. Foremost of these, in addition to C.B., were F. E. Smith, created Lord Birkenhead in 1919, and John Simon, both of whom became Lord Chancellor. All three continued to meet after their Oxford days, Birkenhead and Simon visiting the *Mercury* and becoming Vice-Presidents – in effect members of the Board of Governors. Of the three men, C.B. made the greatest initial impression in public life. He had come to the fore as a sportsman while still only sixteen, playing for the London Casuals in the F.A. Cup. For the next four years he appeared with them, and with the Corinthians and Southampton, in matches against most of the professional clubs. It was, perhaps, a tribute to his school that their star pupil was allowed to go so far afield. In and out of school, C.B. brought credit to his tutors.

During his time at Oxford C.B. rose to be president of the athletics team and captain of the cricket and football teams – honours that seemed bound to accrue to a man who had won blues in all these sports while still only a freshman. A blue in rugby only eluded him when an injury kept him from the critical game with Cambridge. His tremendous physique was captured in a photograph taken of him to illustrate a book on human anatomy for artists written by Arthur Thomson, Professor of Human Anatomy at the university.

Of all C.B.'s sporting triumphs as an undergraduate the one which brought him greatest fame was the long jump at Iffley Park in March 1893, when he equalled the world record of 23 ft 6½ ins. Various stories are told to illustrate his nonchalance in such matters. One tells of his smoking a cigar in the groundsman's hut when the event got under way. He put it down, pulled off his sweater, ran out to equal the record, and then went back to his still smouldering cigar.

After leaving Oxford, C.B. lived precariously in London for a year, which was interrupted by a tour of South Africa to play cricket with a party got together by Lord Hawke. At Oxford he had begun his career as a sports writer with articles in the London papers, but the return on these early efforts could hardly have constituted a proper living. Much later he revealed that he had left home for good when he went to Repton. In his own words, 'From that day onwards, the attention of my parents being otherwise occupied, I found for myself.'[3] Now more than at any other time in his life he had to find for himself. A roll of honour in the Repton chapel describes him as 'sportsman and scholar'. Somehow he had to make a living in a world in which by education, inclination and popular demand he was the personification of the English gentleman – cultured, urbane, civilised, the acme of good manners – but, like Beatie's father, restricted when it came to the ways of making money. In the annual match at Lords between Gentlemen and Players he wanted, above all, to come down the front steps of the pavilion with the Gentlemen, and not out of the side door with the Players.

His first job was as a schoolmaster at Charterhouse, starting in the Oration Quarter (Michaelmas term) of 1896. He did not take his duties very seriously, and spent a great deal of time in a large barn standing before a set of wickets and getting boys to hurl balls at him as hard as they possibly could, so that he could practise endlessly the skills he displayed with such nonchalance and seemingly unrehearsed ease on the cricket fields of England.[4] Aptly enough, he left Charterhouse in the Cricket Quarter of 1898 and went straight to the *Mercury* and marriage with Beatie.

Charles Hoare's passion for cricket undoubtedly brought C.B. into the same orbit. It seems fairly certain that they met when Charles invited C.B. to play at the *Mercury*. Beatie's uncle, Nigel Kingscote, was on the committee of the M.C.C., so Charles would not be welcome at Lords, but the leading figures in sport could come to him. And an invitation to the *Mercury* would have been difficult to refuse, coming as it did from a man of immense wealth who could entertain his guests lavishly and, for all the scandal attached to his name, was known to be 'well connected'.

It was widely believed among people who knew the Frys that they met in 1895, and that immediately on coming down from Oxford C.B. became secretary to the ship, an appointment that was regarded as a form of patronage, enabling him to take time off to pursue his career in sport in exchange for nominal duties; and that three years of friendship with Beatie, meeting her almost daily when he was not away playing games, mellowed into romance and then marriage. As we have seen, there was no secretaryship, and C.B. spent two years at Charterhouse. Another embellishment to the story tells of their having run away from Charles to get married: Charles then sent them a telegram – 'All is forgiven. Come back' – after which, so the story goes, they lived together as a happy trio. This again is unlikely – at least the notion of their living as a trio – as Charles had moved from Hamble to Hall Place, while C.B. and Beatie, when they did indeed get married, moved into Glenbourne, a house in West End, a few miles from Hamble, in what is now a suburb of Southampton.

Nothing seemed less likely than the union between the handsomest man in England and the sturdy woman in Hamble – thirty-six, greying, with her cropped hair and mannish clothes. By the standards of her class, Beatie was marrying 'beneath' her. She was an aristocrat; C.B. came from a middle-class family that would not expect one of its members, least of all a man, to marry someone who was related, directly or by marriage, to the likes of the Duke of Beaufort, the Marquess of Cholmondeley, and Lord Bathurst. On their marriage certificate, under the heading of 'rank or profession of father', C.B. entered 'civil engineer', while Beatie wrote simply 'gentleman'.

If they differed markedly in appearance and origins, they were also distanced by intellect. C.B. was a brilliant Oxford graduate, with an acute mind that absorbed without effort whatever subject took his fancy. When, in December 1908, he became Captain Superintendent of the *Mercury* in succession to Charles Hoare, his academic subjects listed in the staff records were 'Greek, Latin, Moral Philosophy, Ancient History, French, German, Spanish, Mathematics, Physics and Naval History'.[5] Beatie had never been to school in her life, never mind university, and appeared incapable of writing even coherent English. As her husband's interests were expanding, hers were contracting, making the ship the centre of all her energies.

They might have found common ground in a shared interest in outdoor pursuits, but for Beatie the outdoors was the ship and the waters of the Solent and the Channel, demanding a love of the outdoors for its own sake, whereas for C.B. an open stretch of sky was incomplete without an audience to watch and applaud his activities. Beatie was becoming reclusive. C.B. was a showman all his life.

As to why they got married, only they could have answered such a question, and neither of them left any record behind. C.B. had the opportunity to do so in his autobiography, *Life Worth Living*, but said nothing about their meeting, courtship, marriage or the nature of their relationship thereafter. A cynical version was that Charles Hoare persuaded C.B. to marry the lady in order to protect her from the icy blasts of society after his, Charles's, death. C.B. in return would have a sinecure for life, the captaincy of the *Mercury*, which his wife would run for him. It could be argued that she, who had flouted society for so long, married at last for the sake of respectability. However, there may have been much less of a gulf between the newly-weds than appeared on the surface. If C.B. was the Superman of late Victorian England, Beatie was the Superwoman, the fearless rider to hounds whose skill on horseback as much as her striking looks and charisma had attracted one of the richest men in England. At the *Mercury* C.B. would have seen her prowess in another element, as she rowed and sailed on the river with practised skill. She might even have surprised him by swinging aloft, 'over the port rigging, at the top by the futtock shrouds, avoiding lubbers' hole'. By comparison the other women he could have married might have seemed effete.

Their characters, if different, were complementary. C.B. was a man of action, but only in the public arena in which he enjoyed so much success. Away from the public gaze he was elegant, witty, brilliant – but not practical. Beatie, one suspects, would not have wanted a practical person to share the niche she had created for herself, someone with whom she might have to argue about the practicalities of running the ship. The fact that his wife was older than him might well have appealed to C.B. Together they wrote a pallid novel called *A Mother's Son*, and the title may hint at the sheltering role that the older Beatie played for her young husband, protecting him at times from the demands of a public that craved greater and still greater achievements from its idols.

The marriage took place on 4 June 1898. Their first child, Charis, was born in February 1899; they had two more children, Stephen Hope, who was born the following year, and Faith, who was born in 1910, when Beatie was forty-eight. To their first home at West End they took with them Beatie's children by Charles – Sybil, now in her teens, and Robin, though in fact he spent most of his time at boarding school.

For the next ten years Charles controlled the *Mercury*, commuting from West Meon to Hamble, while C.B. stayed in the wings as far as the ship was concerned, and Beatie played a less dominant role there, awaiting the time when she would take over. It was a time which Stephen recalled with pain and bitterness when he spoke about it a few months before his death in 1979. He was left at Glenbourne with servants and to the untender ministrations of his half-sister, while his father pursued a busy life in the public eye, and his mother continued her obsession with 'her ship'.

Life in the public eye included the zenith of C.B.'s cricketing career in partnership with Kumar Shri Ranjitsinhji, Jam Sahib of Nawanagar – 'Ranji', as the public called him. They vied with each other in setting new batting records: in 1901 C.B. scored 3147 runs in first-class cricket, including six centuries in successive innings. He also continued to play football at national level.[6] He was not in the least modest about his performance. In his autobiography he describes the great clubs he played against in 1902, when Southampton were fighting for the Cup: Spurs on their own ground and then at a replay in Reading, in which they beat the League Champions;

Liverpool, at the Dell; a semi-final against Notts Forest at Totten-
ham; a final against Sheffield United at Crystal Palace which ended
in a draw; and then a replay which Sheffield won. He concluded:

Having played in the said final on Saturday, I played in a first-class cricket match
on the following Monday – for W.G.'s London County Eleven against Surrey at
the Oval – and made 78 runs and got some wickets.
 Where is Don Bradman?
 Whatever else he has done he has never played Cup-tie or League football.[7]

Meanwhile Beatie continued to appear at the *Mercury*, though her
role for the time being was secondary to that of Wilfred Hoare. She is
seldom mentioned in letters and other accounts of life on the ship at
this time. In the summer she went to cricket matches with her
husband, but when he was playing at Lords she would sit with the
public most of the time, rather than exercise her right to be with her
husband in the pavilion.

Charles Hoare was now in the last decade of his life, freed from his
former mistress but not unconcerned about her. Within the ship
things went on as before, with Wilfred Hoare sharing the
administration with his father. The religious activities, which had
become so important, found a place of their own when Charles
designed and built a chapel. Previously, services had been held in the
Building, a temporary altar being provided on a platform balanced
between the front of the stage and the balustrade between the
orchestra pit and the audience. The new chapel was built of wood
clad in metal, with the sheets of metal hammered on to the
overlapping planks to retain the impression of a timber construction.
(It was dedicated to St Agatha, reputedly a Sicilian woman of
aristocratic descent: she had been pursued by Quintian, a man of
consular rank, who caused her death by torture when she refused his
advances.) An Anglican priest was employed as a permanent chaplain
to the ship, and the full ritual of the church was celebrated daily. The
atmosphere inside the chapel was one of intense gloom, with the
choir screen and internal fittings and walls varnished or painted in

op left: 1 The young Beatie; *top right*: 2 Margaret Hoare, 1867;
ove: 3 Charles Hoare, M.F.H.

Top: 4 The barque *Illovo*, later the T.S. *Mercury*; *above*: 5 The gun deck, H.M.S. *President*, the dormitory ship from 1916 to 1968.

op: 6 The *Illovo*, main deck, looking aft, *above*: 7 H.M.S. *President*.

8 & 9 C. B. Fry: the handsomest man in England, '. . . a Greek god, so beautiful in face and bod that he might have been wrought by the chisel of Praxiteles, with broad shoulders and narro hips'.

10 & 11 The House. Architect: Charles Hoare.

Top: 12 Charles Hoare, 'the old commander'; *above*: 13 The Building: 'dedicated to minds th
can soar . . .'

p left: 14 Winston Churchill inspects, 1910; *top right*: 15 Boys on parade. Note the shaven
ds; *above*: 16 Visiting royalty: Beatie with H.R.H. the Duke of York.

Top left: 17 C. B. Fry, 1908, the new Captain Superintendent; *top right*: 18 The Captain's Lady; *above*: 19 The Admiral's barge.

dark colours. The windows were of clear glass, but these had been made opaque with coloured images in imitation of stained glass.

The unceasing stream of activity for the boys continued – sailing in the various tenders of the parent ship, drill in all the nautical skills, and games of football, rugby, and cricket at home and away with teams from as far afield as Taunton. They went on forays into the surrounding countryside on bicycles which Charles provided. Occasionally they went by launch to Portsmouth and Gosport to visit the naval training establishment to which most of them were headed. And all the time there was the background of music, in the chapel and the Building, and from bugle calls that punctuated the day, summoning them to meals, bidding them to be still and hear an important order, and to carry on when it was delivered.

Among the visitors to the ship in the opening years of the new century was Harold Begbie, a journalist with the London newspaper, *The Chronicle*. He used to bring with him his daughter Joan, who had been born the year Beatie and C.B. married. In 1980 she remembered these visits with clarity. Boy Mogg was assigned to amuse her, and took her for rides on the model train which Charles had built in the grounds for amusement and to carry stores to the pier for transport by boat to his yachts. Mogg pushed the little girl along in an open truck as he was not allowed to operate the steam engine on his own. Boy L. G. Charles, No. 914, also remembered the Begbies, and how Harold in one of his articles in the magazine *Sunday At Home* described the *Mercury* boys as 'the happiest in England'. In 1974, L. G. Charles, then eighty-two years old and living in retirement in Canada, described life as a *Mercury* boy in 1903. The place was an odd mixture of tough ship and progressive school. The boys still rose at six and went up the rigging in bare feet, but no longer with Beatie to lead them. They came ashore for showers and a breakfast of cocoa and ship's biscuits before attending lessons in classrooms close to the House. There was physical training in a gymnasium and band practice in the Building. At noon everybody returned to the ship for a mid-day meal, and in the afternoon there was rowing, sailing and games. Evenings were full of music, and a long day ended with the 'last post' at nine. When L. G. Charles went on to describe the punishments, the reader might have expected harsh beatings, matching the hardy life style of the boys. Instead the accent was on rewarding good behaviour, with boys able to earn up to a shilling a week if they could avoid 'demerit marks', and to spend it in the tuckshop on 'packets of candies, or allsorts as they were called, jam, jellies, or condensed milk'. The hectic pace of the day was such that deprivation of sleep was the ultimate and most effective punishment. A pail of water was placed on the starboard of the poop deck, an empty pail on the port. After the others were in their hammocks for the night the miscreant had to transfer the contents of one bucket to the other using an egg cup. The night officer put a chalk mark inside the rim of the full bucket, so it was impossible to get away with pouring it into the empty one.

Whereas the younger boys were given the bucket-and-egg-cup punishment, the older ones were 'sent truck from nine to midnight'. L. G. Charles got two sessions of this, one for wagging his ears in chapel and making the other boys laugh, the other when he was working in the galley and slipped on the gangway as he was on his way down to empty some slops into the river. Captain McKenzie, a senior officer, was on his way up at the time, and the boy knocked him overboard. Boy Charles threw him a rope, which was promptly laid across the galley-boy's backside when the dripping officer got on board, a rare instance of corporal punishment, though the offender considered it deserved. The truck is the highest point of the mast, over eighty feet above the deck on a ship the size of the *Mercury*. Boy Charles went up the rigging in the dark, but sneaked up with him a canvas sling he had improvised so that he could tie himself to the top few feet of the mast and doze in safety till the order came for him to return to the deck.

When, in 1974, the old seafarer reflected on his years at the

Mercury he did so with unmistakable pleasure, unaware of the grim place it was to become after the founder had died. He remembered the names of his former shipmates, most of whom he hadn't seen for nearly seventy years ('Hollis, Bonner, Trevor, Mogg') who had been happy with him under Charles Hoare – 'the Old Commander',[8] as he called him.

The Old Commander was still playing cricket for the ship's eleven when he was sixty. The year was 1907. In nearby Southampton the Hampshire County Cricket Club had made him their chairman, an honour which capped a lifetime of devotion to the game. He bought a Rolls-Royce, and in it he went further afield to watch his club play or to collect more ship models for his little museum. Energetic and outgoing, his horizons had expanded in directions unimaginable ten years earlier. At Hall Place, his house in West Meon, he met members of his family and entertained intimate friends, but his former mistress and her husband did not appear there. Harold Begbie stayed there with his wife and children. To Begbie's daughter, Joan, it was a second home, where she even had a small cart drawn by a Shetland pony for her own use. In 1956 a journalist writing in a Southampton paper spoke of 'the white-haired imperious Charles Hoare'[9]; yet in 1980 Joan Begbie spoke of a gentle man, with a deep calm voice, who never raised that voice or his hand to a child.

To Hall Place Harold Begbie brought Arthur Mee, the brilliant Nottingham man whose *Children's Encyclopedia* and *Children's Newspaper* won him so much fame. Together the three men, Begbie, Mee and Charles, talked about education and how much more could be done for children, and Charles heard the journalists advocate ideas which came close to the system he had evolved on the ship where pupils achieved without those in charge having recourse to the repressive measures that were common in the schools of the day.

In the closing weeks of 1907 Charles, rich, admired and now deservedly respected for his work at the *Mercury*, was seen at the ship for the last time. He attended the Prize Day ceremonies on 21 December; two days later he went to Hindhead, ill and in search of a change of air to improve his condition. From thence he went to Brighton, but returned at last to Hall Place in February. In April he took to his bed, stricken with cancer. His son Wilfred, christened 'Father Wilfred' by the Begbie children because of his gentle, priestly manner and appearance, deputised for him at the ship. The leather-bound collection of *Mercury Magazines* for 1908 recorded the minutiae of ship life for that year, interspersed with comments of growing concern about 'their beloved Commander'. Only rarely did the Frys appear in its pages, such as when C.B. gave each boy a present of a book entitled *What Nelson Said* – 'a nice kind present', according to the editor of the magazine.[10]

A peculiarity of the magazine was that each page bore a footnote, usually something hortatory – 'Push forward!' or 'Persevere and never fear' – or some wise apophthegm, such as 'Speak of a man as you find him', or 'Quietness is best'. Reading these footnotes with the knowledge that the editor knew Charles was dying, one is inclined to believe that his failing health was traced in them, even while the main text tried to strike a hopeful note. Thus in January Charles was reported as 'happily now recovering', while the footnote reads 'One is not as soon healed as hurt'. In March he is reported as ill, but we are reminded that 'Love can vanquish death'.

A busy life went on in his absence. In February the chaplain, Mr Blofield, and the chief officer, Mr Bartlett, were out all day with a group of boys, shooting and ferreting. They bagged eight rabbits and a weasel. During some bright days in early March the cricket pitch was rolled and boys tended their own gardens. Their pets – rabbits, mice and bantams – were doing well, but 'one of Moulton's goldfish died'. St Patrick's Day was Wilfred Hoare's birthday and there was a concert of Irish music in the Building to celebrate the day and honour their Commander's son. They gave him three hearty cheers and a chorus of 'For he's a jolly good fellow!' March ended gloomily when Boy Garner Wakefield, No. 966, died in Southampton Hospital after a short illness. His body was placed in the chapel and two boys stayed to watch over him until his funeral the next day. After the service on Saturday afternoon the coffin was placed on a gun carriage drawn by his shipmates. They made their way to the cemetery preceded by a firing party and the band playing 'The Dead March' from *Saul,* so completing a full military funeral, even down to the volleys fired over the open grave.

April was cold, and there was a confusion of blossom and unseasonable snow. In the magazine the editor, on behalf of the boys, addressed himself to Charles, who was sure to get a copy: 'they want you back, sir, they miss you . . . they love you.'

There were rehearsals that month for a performance of three scenes from Verdi's *Il Trovatore.* Easter Sunday fell on the 19th, and they sang the 'Hallelujah Chorus' from Handel's *Messiah* in chapel after the evening service.

May began with cricket matches; there was much excitement on the 16th when two yachts, the *Barbara* and *Allegro,* went aground in the Hamble River and the boys helped to refloat them.

Charles's birthday fell on 18 May. Beatie, aware how close he was to death and unable to visit him in Hall Place, made a gesture which would tell him of her love and sense of grief. She gave him a present of a sick communion set. This was delivered to the house at Hamble, where it was immediately taken to the chapel and placed in the Tabernacle on the high altar. The set, as its name implies, was used to take communion to the sick or to give the last rites of the Church to someone who was dying, the priest obtaining from the Tabernacle the consecrated elements of the ritual and the vessels of the set in one small container – a box for the bread, a bottle filled with wine, a chalice and a patten, all made of silver. It was used that same week to give the last rites to Charles.

He lay in a bedroom with four windows through which he could see a copper beech, with all its portents of spring's early promise, summer's fulfilment, autumn's mellow harvest, and stark winter that ends the cycle – and yet begins another. At the foot of his bed was a little kneeling desk. Beyond this, on the wall, was a crucifix with palms on either side, remnants of that year's Easter celebrations. Here the set was used, bearing him not just the last rites of the Church, but the love of the woman who had transformed his life.

Charles died at 9.30 on the morning of 22 May, four days after his birthday, a pale thin, wasted shell of the powerful man he had once been. The May edition of the ship's magazine carried a description of him as he had been before illness overcame him. Beatie had composed the dedicatory lines which appeared on the wall of the building which includes the words 'To hearts that can beat for others'. The echo of this phrase in the verbal portrait of Charles suggests that Beatie was its author:

Height 6ft. 1in., of noble width in proportion, two good feet carried him, he himself used to say one of his legs was shorter than the other, consequently he walked a little bit late. His hands were always flat and thin rather delicate long-fingered sensitive hands. His chest was abundant and gave his splendid heart room to beat for all. Here was a personality who walked straight on, with a round head crowned with pure white hair. When well his was a rosy face, an absolute gentle firm mouth with two deep lines on either side, a pair of shrewd observant blue eyes set very deep and overhung with the bushiest golden eyebrows. Two well-set ears, which heard every sound, and a beautiful dear kind forehead furrowed with deep lines and a frown.[10]

Tears were shed for him on the ship and at his funeral, when he was buried in West Meon churchyard. Eighteen boys acted as pall bearers, and the thousandth boy to enter the ship walked immediately behind the coffin. C.B. was there, but not Beatie. A simple Celtic cross was later put on the spot, on a rise of ground south and a little east of the church. On it were inscribed his name and the dates of his birth and death. Nothing else. An appropriate epitaph might have been a footnote from the *Mercury* magazine: 'Life is a long lesson in humility'.

How can one sum up this extravagant character? It is not going too far to suggest that he was a peculiar mixture of paradoxes, half bluster and half quintessential Victorian refinement, a man who spent the early part of his life ruining other people's lives, obliquely or otherwise, but who mellowed into middle-aged kindliness. Thirty of these years were spent with Beatie. Their life together seems to us to be curiously public, until one remembers that our only mementoes are newspapers, law reports and the fading memories of the very old: they left no letters or private documents. Although we know only by hearsay what made them tick, one tribute does remain to the intensity of their regard for each other: the episode in Cecily Hill House, when they wept before Arthur Sumner and his efforts to prise them apart.

Publicly Charles had run the gauntlet of society's disdain, to be followed by years of devotion to the ship: the two periods of his life were united by his passion for the girl he had met on the hunting fields of Gloucestershire. His love for her was so circumspect that he may indeed have colluded in her union with C. B. Fry, bringing the two together so that Beatie, the 'fallen woman', would be sheltered from the scorn of society after his death. It was a union which, in denying him her company for ten years, gave him time and space in which to make some kind of peace with himself and with the world. In the end, though much of the damage he had done was irreversible, he won through to such a surprising degree of respect from all sides that his obituarists could honestly describe him as a humble and compassionate man. One of them, attempting to find words to describe a man who was so generous with his life, as well as with his money, wrote that 'It was the poor who loved him so. Them he understood so completely. Here was a socialist, who carried social-ism right up to the front with majesty.'[11] The young coachman, the 'gallant Master of Fox-hounds', as he was so often called in hunting reports, the banker who had tried to burn money faster than the firm could make it, had come a long way.

His will was long and labyrinthine. He left an estate of the gross value of £234,256. All his children were provided for. Sybil and Robin, his children by Beatie, were as well provided for as those born to his wife, Margaret. To his daughter, Agatha, he left Hall Place, the house in which he died. He exercised his right to appoint one of his sons to a partnership in the bank in Fleet Street, but none of them took it up. Ralph, Robin and Reginald were abroad, and Wilfred, who had helped him run the ship, had shown little interest in the family business. It was revealed that as far back as 1886, the year the V.W.H. split, Charles had set up trust funds for Beatie and Sybil, the incomes from which they would receive after his death. No figures were given, but in 1936 Beatie was able to make her own will, leaving investments and property that reflected his generosity. While Beatie's monetary legacy from the will was a mere – but discreet – £300, the entire contents of the House were hers for life, to be passed on after her death to Robin and Sybil. In the unlikely event of the *Mercury* being closed or sold to other people, Beatie was to have the value of the theatre – £1360, the amount it had cost to build.

Despite his concern for the security of his former mistress there is an interesting codicil to the will. He had bought a house in Salcombe in Devon for 'Mary Beatrice Perch (widow)' for £1800, a sum out of all proportion to the figure one might leave to a loyal servant or housekeeper. James McGavin, for example, got an annuity of £20. Had Charles found someone to comfort him in his declining years, someone less overpowering than the formidable Beatie?

There was a long clause in the will in which the future of the *Mercury* was discussed. Charles intended that it should have money from his estate to cover the running costs for two years, during which time his trustees should try to find 'some public body or institution or some person or persons to take over the said training ship', together with his collection of ship models and marine artefacts. It had been hoped that a firm legacy in favour of the ship and the people running it would assure the future of the whole enterprise. At first glance this reservation is puzzling. When these details of the will were published there was a brief flurry of legal wrangling, from which C.B. emerged as a suitable 'public person', able at least to run the ship for the two years covered by its late founder. Within six months, aided by a newly formed governing body, C.B. had collected £2000 in subscriptions and donations, enough to persuade the High Court to establish the *Mercury* as an educational charity under his direction. He described these events in detail in his autobiography, but omitted to mention that, whatever his reservations about leaving money to run the ship, and even supposing his feelings had cooled towards Beatie, Charles had said in his will that 'I particularly recommend that my trustees do employ the said Beatrice Holme Fry . . . as manager . . . of the said training ship either for such remuneration as my trustees may think proper or without remuneration.' Her husband's role in this was to provide the cover under which a woman would command an all-male establishment, and his reward was a life-long sinecure and the freedom to enjoy his life as cricketer, journalist and public figure. He now had all the trappings of a 'gentleman' – a twenty-five room mansion luxuriously furnished, spacious grounds, a Rolls-Royce, and even, to begin with, a butler and servants. He could entertain in style his wide circle of acquaintances – F. E. Smith, John Simon, the Churchills, Kipling, Baden-Powell, Lord Halifax and many more. In time he would pay a bitter price for all this luxury, but to begin with all he had to do was let Beatie run everything as Charles had intended.

9 – *The Gun*

Changes were bound to take place when C.B. and his wife moved from Glenbourne to the official residence of the Captain Superintendent of the TS *Mercury*, but for a year at least the brisk but friendly atmosphere which had been the hallmark of Charles Hoare survived.

In *The Captain*, one of two boys' magazines published at the time and edited by C.B., an article appeared about the ship written by A. B. Cooper, who had stayed in the House as a guest. Dated May 1909, it describes a household as opulent as any of the great country houses of the time. The boys seem a jolly lot, moving at a lively pace through an exciting routine in their novel surroundings with the beautiful barque-rigged sailing vessel on the river, and the spacious shore establishment dominated by the magnificent theatre – the whole, ashore and afloat, referred to simply as the *Mercury*. There is a suitably flattering portrait of C.B. extolling his charm, erudition and commanding good looks, and a short aside on the character of his wife: 'Mrs Fry . . . is the soul of things. She has the loving heart, wise brain, and the kindly eyes, which see and understand, which feel and know, which plan and sympathise.'[1] This may have been an oblique way of informing the reader that Beatie was the guiding force behind the running of the place, and the time was swiftly coming when none of the warm adjectives would apply, at least not in the minds of the young people who were about to feel the full blast of her direct rule. She may, for all they knew, have been loving, wise and kindly, but if so these traits were well concealed.

A photograph of her taken about this time conveys much of the character found by Lytton Strachey in the face of another formidable

lady, Florence Nightingale. There is the same 'serenity of high deliber-
ation in the scope of the capacious brow'. The eyes reflect the 'sign of
power', 'the traces of a harsh and dangerous temper' that Strachey
read into the face of his subject. 'There was humour in the face, but
the curious watcher might wonder whether it was humour of a very
pleasant kind; might ask himself . . . what sort of sardonic merriment
this same lady might not give vent to, in the privacy of her chamber.'[2]

For a year at least C.B. exercised some authority, and thereafter
took part in the day-to-day running of the place when it did not
interfere with his public life as sportsman, journalist, and *bon viveur*,
much in demand in the homes of the great and the famous. In
January 1909, a month after he formally took up office as Captain
Superintendent, a future Commander RN, A. E. Horrell, joined
the ship. In his eighties Horrell retained clear and affectionate
memories of a man who could take a class on most subjects and
inspire his pupils by his command of them. Sadly these occasions
were few and irregular, but the possibility that the permanent
member of staff might look up from his work to find C.B. hovering in
the doorway, ready and willing to take over the class in an instant,
served to keep the standards high. When he was at the *Mercury* in
1914, Reggie Sinfield, Boy No. 1391, saw the great man teaching
seamanship and signals, but C.B.'s enthusiasm for teaching of any
kind, other than on the playing field, seems to have been shortlived.
Certainly it had evaporated by the end of the First World War.
Inevitably the sporting life of the ship received most of his attention –
it was pretty openly admitted, as it might have been at a public school,
that a new instructor or even a carpenter taken on the staff might get
the job in preference to other applicants if he could play cricket. In
the summer boys queued up at the nets to bowl to one of the greatest
batsmen ever to take the field. There was promise of payment if they
could bowl him out: a sixpence was balanced on the top of each
stump instead of bails, and whoever knocked them off could keep
them. C.B. seldom lost his money.

For a select few there was a chance to play in his team at a weekend match that might include some of the finest players in the world, such as 'Plum' Warner, Philip Head and Ranjitsinhji. It is not surprising that some boys developed a life-long passion for the game. Bill Mobsby, Boy No. 1846, who took a sixpence or two at the nets, managed to return to the *Mercury* in later years to play cricket, and Reggie Sinfield went on to play at county level and to achieve fame as the man who bowled out Bradman in the 1938 Nottingham Test.

As her husband's enthusiasm for the steady routine of running the ship declined, Beatie took firmer control – as Charles Hoare had always assumed she would.

To outsiders the first dramatic change came about in 1910, with the success rate among boys passing advance class soon after entering the Royal Navy shooting up from four or five a year to fifty or more out of the sixty going annually into the service.[3] Passing advance class meant that a recruit had arrived with the skills he would otherwise have to acquire before training as a specialist in one of the many departments of a warship – in seamanship, rifle drill, signals, and swimming, together with competency in the basic subjects of education. On the *Mercury* the curriculum was narrowed down so as to achieve success in these skills, not just for the glory it might bring to all concerned, but because it paid. The ship received a bounty from the Admiralty, a sum of money that varied over the years from £15 to £25 per boy. The Navy had been saved the cost of three months' training, and it was sound economics to reward the agency which had produced these results. In good years C.B. and Beatie had an income of over £1000 a year from this source, a welcome sum even though the finances of the ship were probably less precarious than C.B. liked people to believe.

Narrowing the curriculum meant a shift in emphasis away from that which had prevailed in the earlier years.

Under Charles Hoare life on board had been strongly influenced by his special relationship with the boys in his care. They were like an enormous family that needed a high level of discipline, if only to bring order to lives sometimes spent in crowded conditions, in boats or on the little ship on the river. But there was also room for individuality, with pets and garden plots to look after and bicycles to ride in the lanes outside. Under Beatie all these were abolished. Her regimentation of life on board quickly became total. She had a loathing, containing in it a distinct element of fear, of boys being idle or even momentarily out of her control. If they were not being eternally shunted from one activity to another by her staff, then they had to shunt each other. A group going from the main building to the bucket lavatories – the 'heads', in nautical parlance – at the foot of the playing field would identify, in the absence of a member of staff, the most senior of their number and then allow him to march them to the heads and back. Occasionally the more spirited of their number satirised this aspect of ship's life. Two boys, given permission to use the heads, would decide which was the senior, and he would tell his companion to 'get fell in', call him to attention, and then march his squad of one of its destination, subjecting it to the full barrage of imprecations learned from the ex-naval petty officers who taught them drill – 'You 'orrible lot! Get in step! Pick yer feet up!' This sort of levity was, however, rare.

The element of fear in Beatie's mentality stemmed from the very real danger of the enterprise failing and leaving her at the mercy of a world which still knew too much about her past for comfort. She could quiet these fears by making the ship so successful that her way of life and her livelihood were secure. She could also cut herself off from the world – a device that meant cutting the boys off from it as well. If they wandered into the village or spoke to outsiders they might learn about her past, and thus erode her authority and, worse still, her security. And so began the burden of constraints which weighed heavily on every generation of boys from 1909 until death relieved Beatie of all her earthly worries.

There were other innovations which served to tighten Beatie's grip on everybody. In- and out-going letters were read by her and Sybil. Boys had been numbered from the time the school was founded, if only to serve as a running record of how many had passed through. Now they were addressed by their numbers at all times, wore them conspicuously on the backs of their shirts, and used numbers instead of names even among themselves, if only because an instructor might send for '578', and the messenger would have to know to whom these digits applied.

Curiously enough, in spite of her fears, Beatie entered on two practices which emphatically kept alive memories of Charles Hoare. Every Saturday she and Sybil went in the Rolls to the churchyard in West Meon. They took gardening tools with them, and tended his grave. What Beatie's husband felt about this weekly pilgrimage has not been recorded. This went on for many years and an immediate result of it was that Charles's daughter, Agatha, sold Hall Place and left West Meon for good. To have been deprived of her father in his lifetime had been a burden. To have his grave tended by the woman who was the author of this was intolerable.[4]

The second practice was one of keeping unoccupied the seat Charles had used in the chapel – the middle chair in a row of five, six rows from the front on the south side of the aisle. A shallow bowl of flowers was maintained on it for the next forty-two years.

One of the first problems Beatie had to solve on taking over in 1908 was to find a replacement for the sailing ship *Mercury*, now over forty years old and presenting problems familiar to the owner of any yacht. Repairs and maintenance were costly, so much so that the bills threatened to be greater than the actual value of the ship; and even when they had been completed, its value was inevitably decreasing with age. C.B.'s fame, his Oxford connections and his brilliant circle of acquaintances brought a solution to the problem. He began by reviving an application made by Charles Hoare some years earlier to the Admiralty for a replacement, and was offered HMS *President*, the RNR drill ship. More time went by without anything happening when, in 1914, he received an unexpected visit from the First Lord of the Admiralty, Winston Churchill, accompanied by his brother Jack, Admiral Hood, and F. E. Smith, whom C.B. had known at Oxford. Despite a mere ten minutes' notice, the ship's company was mustered and ready for inspection on their arrival. So impressed was Churchill by the boys and the establishment that he was ready to act on C.B.'s request for the ship, which had been promised six years earlier, to be delivered.[5] Within a few weeks the *President*, formerly HMS *Gannet*, was towed down the Channel by the battleship HMS *Queen* to Portsmouth and then by tug to the Hamble. For two years the two ships dominated the river, the sailing vessel, her elaborate rigging still intact, dwarfed by her neighbour with her high ugly superstructure, though the *President* was in fact only thirty feet longer than the barque.

The sailing ship *Mercury* – the former *Illovo* – was sold in 1916 to a Mr David Petrie for £1250 and was converted into a coal hulk.[6] She was taken from the Hamble River in September to Harland and Wolff's shipyard at Southampton where the work took place. This was the fate of many ships – coal was still the prime source of energy for most powered ships, only a few warships of advanced design being oil-fired. The coal hulks – the Royal Navy called them 'coal haulabouts' – provided a means of storing fuel that was cheap and flexible. Instead of paying to go alongside a wharf to bunker, a steamship would tie up alongside a hulk and take the coal from there. Alternatively, a tug would bring the hulk to the ship where she lay in port, and bunkering took place without interrupting the other activities of loading and discharging cargo on the quay.

Both Beatie and her husband romanticised her life and death. C.B. wrote of her as she had been when she was carrying cargo as 'searching for wind in the China Seas'. In fact her longest journey had been to the coast of East Africa by way of the Cape of Good Hope. Beatie preferred another's words to express her feelings, quoting in every edition of the Prize Day programme for years the lines written by Gregory Robinson, entitled 'The Good Ship'. Robinson was a marine artist of some note who lived in Hamble village. He wrote, 'It is many years since she glided down the straight ways into the grey North Sea, the pride of the man who built her – a ship with a fine entry and a clean run . . .' There follows a passage in which the writer traces her career, coming at last to rest in the Hamble River. Hundreds of boys are trained in her before she is taken to the shipyards to be converted to a coal hulk. Her death is described in anthropomorphic terms. Feeble and old, 'she dipped to the sea, but could not lift, and the waters closed over her'. He concludes:

So she passed into the quiet starlit waters of Memory, there to wait for orders. And there for us she remains until the stars pale to gold; then those orders will come, and she will lay a course for the Islands of the Blessed, there to join company with all good ships and enter the Splendid Haven.[7]

These slightly fanciful words were seized on by Beatie, who could not imagine an ignominious end to the ship that had lain at the heart of her struggle for personal freedom. For the end, as far as it can be traced, was just that. In 1917 she was under tow, loaded with coal, in or near the port of Cardiff, and foundered in a sudden squall when the tow-rope snapped. At a time when the newspapers were crammed with news of a terrible war, the loss of a mere hulk went unnoticed.

With the departure of the old sailing ship most of the daily routine now took place on shore, with meals being served in a new dining hall. More buildings would be added over the years.

When the war ended, forty-six old *Mercury* boys had died in action. Their worth, and the worth of hundreds of others who had served with them, and had been hammered into seaman-like material by Charles or his successor, was recognised by the authorities responsible for awarding service decorations. Beatie was appointed Officer of the Civil Division of the Most Excellent Order of the British Empire in the Birthday Honours List of 1918. As a girl she had never made her debut at Court, as would have been normal for a girl of her background. Now she went to Buckingham Palace to receive her Badge at an investiture held on 29 October. This single event shattered the myth of her joint captaincy with C.B.; the bizarre episodes of her young life were discreetly forgotten, and the doors of the great houses of Gloucestershire opened to her again. Six years later Lord Apsley, the grandson of the sixth Earl Bathurst, was guest of honour at a Prize Day and joined the distinguished list of ship's vice-presidents.

In 1918 recognition came to Robin Hoare, the second of the two children born to Beatie and Charles. After attending the Loretto School in Edinburgh, he had taken a suite at the Berkeley in London – and sent his father the bills. It was probably the gesture of a young man who had been hurt by the discovery of his origins in an age that was extremely uncharitable towards the illegitimate. Old *Mercury* boys, recording their memories in later years, remembered him as an enigmatic youth who owned his own yacht. He would appear on the river mysteriously one day, stay for a week, and just as mysteriously disappear. At last he was packed off to New Zealand, where he stayed for a few years before working his passage home via Valparaiso – where he took charge of a string of polo ponies for delivery to an English port – arriving in time to join the RNVR at the outbreak of hostilities in 1914. Between April and August of 1918 he was awarded the DSC, the DSO, the Albert Medal and a bar to the DSO. His contemporaries described him as a man completely without fear, seeking dangers and going into them against a stream of men fleeing for their lives.

Beatie seemed to wield authority with an even greater confidence after receiving the OBE. The symbol of her authority – appropriately enough – was the gun. A 6-inch breech-loading weapon it was cemented into a low platform in a corner of the gymnasium, its barrel pointing through a gunport which could be opened and closed in much the same manner as the gunports on the *President*. It had been put there for drill purposes, so that teams of boys could gather round to load it with dummy shells, 'fire it', and extract the 'spent' shell cases as they would on the warships they were to join later. In fact it was the centre-piece in the ceremonial floggings which became a feature of ship's life soon after Beatie took over. For ten years the man in charge of floggings was Arthur Ward, known behind his back as 'Sharkey'. He was thirty years old when he joined the staff in 1914.[7] A former petty officer, he had served in the main training establishments of the Royal Navy as a physical training instructor, the hardest of the hard men who ruled the lower deck of the service. He was a short, extremely powerful man, dark-visaged, with a grey, menacing jaw. The subjects he taught were officially listed as 'Seamanship, Swimming, Wrestling (two styles), Fencing and Boxing', but his main function was to be the instrument of Beatie's rule, to thrash (not to put too fine a point on it) the school into submission. In the 1980s men who had suffered under him were bitter in their recollections. Though able, in the evening of their lives, to shrug off the hardships and vicissitudes of decades at sea, they harboured nevertheless a detestation of the man as livid as the weals he had once left on their young bodies.

Beating was the punishment for a wide range of offences. Merely being a nuisance was enough to earn a trip to the gun. For boys who were caught stealing there was no escape, but they were so hungry that they still took the risk, looting the vegetable garden in which their more fortunate predecessors had worked their own plots. Running away was considered the worst offence, so that the boy who most feared the regime was the prime victim of its severity.

Beatie decided who was to be flogged, 'awarding' – her word – up to twenty-four strokes. She left it to Mr McGavin, her chief officer, to announce the news at breakfast. In 1921, for example, No. 1766, J. Isaacs, was awarded twelve strokes across the gun 'for being a General Nuisance'. After breakfast the ship's company marched to the gymnasium and were formed into lines to witness punishment.

Some of their possessions were stored in the building. Their 'ditty' boxes, small wooden containers holding a few personal items, were on racks along two of the walls. Their oilskins were hoisted to the ceiling on clothes racks; one of these was lowered, and a few garments were removed and thrown over the breech mechanism of the gun to protect the genitals of the victim from injury. Meanwhile, Boy No. 1766 was conducted to a changing room where he was made to strip naked and then dress in a pair of thin white cotton trousers. When he entered the gymnasium he walked past his assembled shipmates and mounted the gun platform. He stood facing the gun, the barrel pointing away from his midriff like a huge steel phallus. Behind him and to his right was McGavin, a clipboard in his hand bearing a piece of paper. 'Sharkey' stood to his left, holding a thick, almost inflexible cane with decorative twine wrappings at its extremities.

McGavin read out the charge and the number of cuts. The greater the punishment, the more likely it was Beatie would be present, standing by the main entrance, looking across the heads of the boys to see that it was done. 'Sharkey' ordered the boy to bend over the gun, and on the order 'Carry on!' from McGavin he struck with all his might.

The instant the blow fell 'Sharkey' would decide if his victim could stand the rest without flinching. Often he could not, and the man laid aside his cane and with short cords tied the boy's ankles to rings on the platform, and his wrists to the gun-carriage. 'Sharkey' then took up the cane and continued his work, placing every blow in a different place to maximise the pain. He smirked as he struck, appearing to enjoy his work. He put his full strength into the blows, just as he had when caning grown men in the Navy, even though his victim could be a child as young as eleven or twelve. McGavin dutifully ticked them off on his fly sheet, and Beatie watched impassively. The damage was so appalling that a boy who was 'awarded' twenty-four cuts had to take them in two sessions, a month apart. The grim evidence was there for all to see in the showers the next morning.

Those who could survive without cries or tears, and without the indignity of being tethered like a wild animal, turned on their tormentor and gave him the look of utter contempt they felt he deserved.

When it was all over the boys left the gymnasium in cold fear of the man who had done this thing, and of the woman who licensed him to do it.

C.B. took no part in this, though he appeared to be aware of that which took place under what was ostensibly his own authority. What he could not have envisaged, when he became Captain Superintendent in order to allow his wife to become manager, was that his step-daughter, Sybil Hoare, and his own daughter, Charis, would join her as deputies in the enterprise. In the 1920s, when he was often away for months at a time, the place was run entirely by these women. Sybil policed the establishment, ashore and afloat, on behalf of her mother, and all too often when a boy was spreadeagled over the gun it was on the strength of her reports. The instructors feared her too, resenting the power she exercised over them, but they were helpless before her; yet they pitied her the long hours of drudgery she suffered, working in the laundry, handling the hundreds of garments that were washed every week, and undertaking a host of other menial tasks. Charis worked in the office. She was gentle and more kindly than her half-sister. Boys wrote to her after they left, much as they used to write to her mother in the early days, and Charis answered them like a favourite aunt, concerned about their welfare, applauding success, commiserating failures. Faith was too young to be involved in administration, but as an excellent musician she took part, along with Charis, in the rich musical life of the ship. In common with their mother, none of the three daughters had ever been to school.

Stephen lived in the House immediately after the First World

War, after coming home from serving in the Royal Navy as an engineer officer. He had trained at Osborne, the short-lived naval college on the Isle of Wight, where he was a contemporary of the future Admiral of the Fleet, Lord Mountbatten of Burma, but he disliked the whole business of life at sea, and resented being forced into it by his parents. He made no pretence at being able to order boys about, nor did he have any desire to instruct except on the cricket field or in the theatre, where he too joined in the music-making. His position was unenviable. He had neither his father's brilliance nor his mother's character, and since their interests were elsewhere – his father leading a busy life in the public eye, his mother obsessed with regulating the lives of 'her boys' – he was left to his own devices. For years he lived a shadowy existence with no firm purpose. Had he written his life story it would have been revealing on the subject of what it was like to be the son of formidable parents, and a gentle man in a hard school run entirely by women.

10 – 'Make him bleed!'

By the mid-1920s three decades of care and attention had mellowed the shore establishment from a bleak slope going down to the Hamble to a small park with trees and well-tended gardens. A rough rectangle of forty-five acres was bounded on two long sides by Satchell Lane and the Hamble. Of the remaining sides, the one nearest the village stretched from a letter-box on the lane down to the river, while the fourth separated the grounds from open country, which in those days stretched with little interruption to Bursledon, a couple of miles upstream. A tiny stream bisected the site. On one half stood the buildings, on the other, that nearest Hamble village, the sports field. Charles Hoare's 'Institution' had mellowed into something less harsh with ivy growing up the wall in places, and trees close by which helped to soften the outlines. At the point where the sports field began to slope suddenly down to the river stood the tall signal mast. Near this was a pergola of rustic poles covered in climbing roses which Beatie had planted and which she maintained, as she maintained most of the gardens close to the House. Against the hedge nearest Satchell stood a small cricket pavilion.

In 1980, elderly men who had trained at the *Mercury* vividly recalled their experiences of Beatie in 1920. Ernest Walker represented the new type of boy who entered the ship after the war. They were no longer 'improved street arabs' to be saved from 'temporal and eternal ruin'. Many were the sons of resourceful parents who were ambitious for their children, and went about the business of realising those ambitions with determination. Ernest's background was comfortably middle-class, with family money coming from ownership of textile mills and Manchester cotton-broking.

He could have gone to public school, but chose instead the *Mercury*, as did many others, because of the aura shed on it by C.B.

In August 1920 Mr and Mrs Walker and their son arrived by taxi at the gate on Satchell Lane nearest the ship's chapel. They walked along the drive which took them behind the House. Coal had been delivered, and a pile lay on the ground by the basement hatch. They heard the noise of shovelling from below and called for directions to the office. A woman appeared, holding a shovel. She was dressed in a navy blue jacket and skirt. She told them the way, and when they reached the place they were met by Charis, who was then joined by her mother, still grimy from her efforts in the basement. At fifty-eight Beatie was as strong as a horse and ready to turn her hand to anything.

If their first feelings for the lady were of admiration, these were dispelled by the events of the next half hour or so. In his seventies Ernest remembered the occasion:

She spoke to my father briefly, then called to a passing boy and told him to take me to the gymnasium. This he did, carrying my suitcase. In the gymn was an officer, I seem to remember that it was Mr Reid. He told me to tip everything out of my case, and then he began stencilling my number on my clothes. He produced a kit-bag and tipped out its contents: a complete naval uniform. He told me to change into it. This I did, then he sent for a chair. He told me to sit in it, and taking one of my towels to put round my shoulders, he proceeded to clip off every hair on my head! Yes, I began to weep quietly. I was only fourteen years of age, and this was my first time away from home. I felt I was being reduced to the state of a convict. When this was finished he told the boy to take me back to the office.

When my parents saw me my mother burst into tears at the sight of my hairless head. In those far off days hair was kept short, but now I looked as if my head had been shaved. My father demanded of Mrs Fry the reason for this barbarism, to which he was told more or less to mind his own business, that it was essential in the maintenance of cleanliness for all boys to have their hair short. My father observed that my hair was not just short – there was none! But he was not enlightened further, and very soon the time came for my parents to leave. We made our farewells amidst more tears, and I could see that my father was furious; he felt he had handed me over to something more akin to a Borstal institution than a naval training school. He told me to write and let him know how things were, but I was never able to do this, because Mrs Fry told me that a letter containing criticism would be destroyed, and I would be severely punished.[1]

The school year was divided into two terms, from mid-January to early July, and from late August to mid-December. In the term beginning January 1921, Walker reached such a low ebb that he asked to speak to C.B. The face at the office window demanded reasons, but he would not give them. At last he was allowed to enter the great man's office and was received with kindness, heard with sympathy, and given gentle words of encouragement and a look of such compassion that he was able to return to the ranks and see out the long dreary term to the end. When he got home his health had been so impaired that the family doctor instructed his parents not to allow him to return. Ernest went on to a career of high adventure, serving in the RAF, prospecting for gold in Canada, exploring in the Arctic, organising his own Antarctic expedition (only to have it frustrated by the start of the Second World War), fighting in Crete, being captured by German paratroopers and then proving so habitual an escaper that his captors often had to put him in chains; but for now he had had enough.

The pace then as always was unrelenting, with 'Sharkey' Ward to the fore in the race to keep the boys not just busy but harassed to the point of exhaustion. He would take a crew of boys in a cutter down to Southampton Water and back, driving them as if they were able-bodied seamen and not mere boys. He strutted up and down the boat, from thwart to thwart, the tiller in his hand as a club to beat them about the shoulders when he thought they were slacking. On shore he was in charge of boxing lessons in the little cricket pavilion. The lessons were simple and direct, which is to say that he took on the whole class, one at a time, and battered them. Only once did he get his come-uppance. A boy who could take no more got up from the floor, dazed and bloodied, and grabbed a broom that was propped against the wall. He brought the handle down on 'Sharkey's' head, a smashing blow that cut him to the bone and required twelve stitches to close it. The boy went to the gun, but perhaps wisely 'Sharkey' never laid a finger on him again.

His reign went on for several more years. In September 1922, he was administering a 'shake-up' on Beatie's instructions, making the boys run round and round the playing field carrying rifles over their heads, or at full arm stretch in front of them with one hand, and then in the other. When boys began to collapse, 'Sharkey' beat them with a length of knotted rope and forced them to keep going. When Boy No. 1927, Geoffrey Petch, collapsed there was no response to the blows or the orders. He was carried to the verandah, and from thence by ambulance to hospital, but was found to be dead on arrival.

There was no ceremony for the dead boy, no night in the chapel with his shipmates to watch over him, no gun carriage, no bugle calls or volley over his open grave. In the ship's log there were a few laconic words: 'Died whilst under training at the RHS Infirmary, Southampton. He is buried at Hull.'[2] Dreadful though this episode might seem in modern eyes, it created surprisingly little disturbance at the time. It was not reported in the newspapers, for example. 'Sharkey' had been an instructor at HMS *Ganges*, the land-based training ship which was on the peninsula between the rivers Orwell and Stour, a few miles south-east of Ipswich. There he had seen boys of fifteen and sixteen die 'whilst under training'. They lie buried in the naval cemetery attached to Shotley parish church, side by side with sailors and marines killed in action in ships off the coast of East Anglia.

The most incredible aspect of life on the *Mercury* was that much of the punishment handed out was for unspecified offences. The 'shake-up' that killed Petch was a sharp reminder of who was in charge as much as anything else, but if an explanation were given it was that boys were getting 'slack' and needed something to make them 'taut' again. In the verandah Beatie kept a notice board with a list of defaulters. It was up to each boy to read this every day to discover if he was in trouble. The list merely indicated the offenders and the punishment, never the offence, even supposing there was one. To appear on the list meant a spell of running barefooted round a flinty track in the vicinity of the signal mast where boys waited for their turn at the heads. Up to the early 1920s, the mast itself was occasionally used for a variant of the punishment on the old sailing ship of 'going truck till midnight'. The ship's company would assemble in the morning to see one of their number, dressed in thin cotton clothes, forced to climb to the cross-trees, over fifty feet above the ground, where he stayed for the whole day without food or drink. It was not unknown for a boy in winter to become so cold and frightened by the end of the day that his mates had to climb the rigging to help him down.

Another Old *Mercury* Boy who recorded his experiences on the ship was Commander Henry Gardner, who had a distinguished career in the Fleet Air Arm from which he retired to a house in Victoria, British Columbia. When he died in 1979 his widow presented the manuscript of his unpublished autobiography to the National Maritime Museum, Greenwich.[3] Like Ernest Walker, he recalled life on the ship in the early 1920s, having gone there partly with the assistance of a Council Scholarship. His father earned £150 a year, but so highly did he value the prospect of his son getting the start in a naval career which the *Mercury* seemed to offer that he willingly made the sacrifices needed to kit out his son and to pay the fees outstanding after the scholarship money had been spent.

Young Gardner's first encounter with Beatie was marginally less traumatic than that of Ernest Walker. In the company of his mother he presented himself at the office and 'through the window there peered a large red face framed in short grey hair'. The face addressed him 'in a booming baritone voice' and sent him off to change into uniform and have his hair shorn. Once again there followed the insensitive business of presenting the boy to his mother, who was predictably aghast at the transformation which had taken place.

What Gardner experienced in eighteen months on the ship was so disturbing that, like everybody else, he found the Royal Navy by comparison rather lax. He vividly recalled the first hour of the day which was spent on 'clean ship', scrubbing and polishing with the fervour of those who knew that Beatie and Sybil would inspect their work, and that the gun awaited those whose work was unsatisfactory. As a boy he could only guess at how heavily the authority of these women weighed on the men who worked for them. Their children often had to play in the ship's grounds so as to get a glimpse of their fathers in term time, and their wives endured loneliness comparable to that of women whose husbands were at sea, for there was pressure on the staff, especially the senior men, to work inordinately long hours. Since the boys had to be driven relentlessly from six in the morning until nine at night, somebody had to be on hand all the time to see that this was done. It was not enough merely to be on duty. They had to provide visible proof of having pushed the boys to the limit. An instructor called 'Stumpy' Childs had the boys scraping the surface of the deck under their hammocks with their bare hands for any stray bits of blanket wool that had escaped the brooms on the days when the decks were not scrubbed – a process called 'fluffing'. The men invented new punishments, or turned mundane tasks into something so exhausting that it constituted a punishment. Billy Reid, a seamanship instructor as well as being handy with the clippers, devised a senseless exercise called 'luffs and tackles'. A ship's tackle, used for lifting heavy weights, was spread out on the ground and, instead of weights, boys were attached to it, pulling against each other in a hopeless tug-o'-war, while Reid set about them with a rope's end.

The dining hall, which might have provided an oasis of relief in the avalanche of activity that constituted the day, became instead a battlefield. On every table lay a utensil which symbolised the daily struggle for survival – a soup ladle, heavily dented. As the longest implement to hand, it was used by the section leader as a club to beat anyone who stepped out of line by not working hard enough to satisfy the impossibly high standards expected of them here as in every other part of the ship. Something as simple as singing grace, usually a verse from an infant hymn, had to be done to perfection, with several repeats if need be, while the food on the table got cold. Once seated, the utensils they ate from were a further source of dismay. In the 1920s porridge was eaten from wooden bowls with wooden spoons. To those who needed every ounce of food going they were an abomination. It was difficult, short of using fingers or licking the bowl, to get every last vestige of the food off the wooden surface and into the mouth. The bulk of each meal – a sort of dietary backbone – consisted of a long loaf of white bread, though for reasons never made clear there might be a loaf and a half or, very rarely, even two loaves to a mess, the name given to the group of twelve boys at each table. One person cut the bread into slices with the ritual precision of one who knew he would get the last pick and, if he miscalculated, the smallest slice.

Once out of the dining hall and on to the next stage of the day's routine, the hazards multiplied. The standards of dress and appearance were, like everything else, almost impossibly high, in some instances because the means of achieving them were always in short supply. For example, having perfect bootlaces was absolutely essential, but if a lace broke or somebody stole it, it could not be replaced. It was forbidden to go to the village to buy another pair, and no laces were sold on the ship, yet no excuse of any kind was accepted if a boy reached an inspection with these items missing. Punishment followed as night follows day. The misery bred by what was no more than a minor inconvenience was incalculable. The loss of a lace reverberated through the company as the victim hunted for another, and if successful, either by violent appropriation or simple theft, set off a chain reaction in the ranks. It was almost as if Beatie had set them at each other's throats, men and boys alike, as part of a scheme to dominate their lives at all times.

Even the few moments of leisure were beset with hazards. It was forbidden to slump down, to loll, to fall asleep or simply 'cave in' when a rare break in the routine occurred. In summer, when C.B. included a couple of boys in a cricket team, which otherwise was composed of the top players in the country, the rest were privileged to sit around the edge of the field and watch. They had to sit bolt upright for hours, arms crossed in front of them. They were, as one of their number put it in later years, like rabbits mesmerised before a stoat. Beatie and Sybil kept watch, and the first to waver was the first to get a verbal lashing, with the promise of something nasty to follow from the long list of punishments available. The cricket pitch itself had been brought to perfection by miscreants, lugging a heavy roller backwards and forwards over it until they were limp with fatigue.

Surprisingly, there was the occasional moment of relief from all this. Colin Ridge – the boy who had cracked 'Sharkey' over the head with the broom handle – remembered Thursdays, when the tuck shop opened and sixpence would buy a pound of broken biscuits. Afterwards there was letter writing followed by an evening in the Building:

At six o'clock we'd march into the theatre and sit in dead silence with folded arms.

Suddenly the lights would be extinguished and there on the screen amidst rapturous applause would appear the caption 'Harry Burrel, a real regular fellow and owner of the Bar H Ranch'. If Stephen Fry's arm ached from hand cranking the 35mm projector for two hours he had succeeded in making Thursday a happy day.[4]

Time spent in the Building was treasured not only for the film shows, but because it brought the boys into contact with men who differed markedly from the ex-petty officers who formed the bulk of the instructional staff. The bandmasters were also ex-servicemen, usually from Royal Marine bands, but their discipline, in the sense of mastery of a given subject, put them in a totally different category. To begin with, their subject gained them special favour in Beatie's eyes, since music was associated with her spiritual aspirations. Nor could it be presented with the shouts, insults and blows that accompanied a lesson in gunnery or boat drill. C.B. was to claim in later years that the emphasis on music was a key factor in raising academic standards – 'you can see dull boys growing intelligent under its influence.' He went on to remark, 'This is not a matter of supposition. I have noted any number of cases where, the moment a boy began to improve in music, he began also to improve in all other subjects, especially mathematics.'[5]

Probably there was some truth in this, but C.B. left out of his reckoning that for music to be successfully taught on the *Mercury* a comfortable relationship between teacher and pupil had to prevail. If a boy felt he was being bullied he ran no risk if he stopped making progress in the subject: he was merely passed over as tone deaf. Inevitably a large number of boys responded to treatment that differed drastically from that experienced on the parade ground or on the river. Success led to other pleasant diversions. The tradition of the school band playing on bandstands in the locality continued. Together with the Fry children, boys entered competitions in music festivals, usually in Winchester; they returned with prizes in music and country dancing, and had their successes recorded in local newspapers as well as in the ship's magazine. R. E. Hutchins, who rose to high rank in the Royal Navy, went even further afield, accompanying Stephen Fry to London. Stephen gave a piano recital in the Rudolf Steiner Hall of music by Debussy, while Hutchins provided visual accompaniment, projecting light on to a screen, the beam bouncing off a tray of water which rippled in time to the music.

For many boys the chapel became a place of sanctuary. There was always an Anglican priest to officiate at the service, and without exception they were kindly men who won respect for their ability to make the chapel a true haven, and for being undaunted by Beatie. One suspects that they tempered the harsh life of the *Mercury*. They had to accept the rule of compulsory church attendance imposed by her, but to a man these priests insisted that attendance at the three-hour long service on Easter Sunday be voluntary and there were to be no recriminations against those who did not attend. Year after year, until the school year was changed and Easter fell in a holiday period, the chapel was packed on that sacred day. Beatie, of course, was there and took the Sacraments, as she did at every opportunity during the rest of the year, always kneeling at the same place by the altar rail; but for once nobody trembled at her presence.

The sports field provided a diversion for some boys, but not as much as it might have done in a conventional school. It used up precious energy, and playing at anything less than full tilt was regarded as a sort of moral crime.

Famous visitors to the ship brought some relief, but they were a mixed blessing. It was exciting to meet, face to face, such heroic figures as Evans of the *Broke* who was in command of HMS *Broke* in 1917, when she rammed a German destroyer at twenty-seven knots or Shackleton, the explorer, who came to see them before his last voyage to the Antarctic, or Dunbar-Naismith, who had taken his submarine through the 'impenetrable' Dardanelles and bombarded Constantinople; on the other hand, even higher standards of excellence were required as far as the appearance of the place was concerned when such visitors were expected.

A frequent visitor in the 1920s, staying for weeks at a time with the Fry family, was Clara Butt, the singer. She appeared to use the House as her base when she was performing at theatres on the south coast, and she often appeared on the stage of the Building. After one of her visits, she left behind her son Victor – reputedly uncontrollable at his public school – who was made to join the ranks as he was said to be in need of discipline. He adjusted cheerfully to the rigours of life in the ranks. The only concession accorded him was a bed in the House instead of a hammock on the dormitory ship.

The Building, the chapel, the playing field, and the famous visitors – these brought some relief or colour to a world of iron discipline. Without them life might have been intolerable.

There was no question of the sick bay of the early 1920s proving a refuge. It was in the hulk of an old yacht hauled up on the river bank next to the pier. A nursing sister lived on board, her cabin in the fore part of the vessel well clear of the river. Her patients lived in the after part which flooded at high tide. The sister had to put on wellingtons when she went to minister to their needs.

It must be admitted that Beatie drove herself as hard as she drove the boys and her staff. She rarely left the premises. She was up before everybody, and in winter she lit the fires in the House herself. She did not rest until 'Last Post' was sounded, and the lights went out on the dormitory ship. She shared some of the hardships inflicted on the boys, sleeping in an unheated room with the window open all the year round. After her death, her room was cleared and a pigeon's nest was found on top of the wardrobe. She did not baulk at physical labour, as Ernest Walker discovered, and was often to be seen engaged in work she could have delegated to a labourer from the village. The War Memorial, the little brick clock tower, was commissioned by her, but she dug the foundations herself. She was in her seventies before she gave up rowing boats on the Hamble, and it was not uncommon for her to go out by herself in a 32-foot cutter, pulling two large oars in a boat designed to be propelled by ten men. E. P. Hunter of Exeter, Gardner's contemporary on the ship, remembers her as being dressed in a long ankle-length red serge skirt, a much-worn cardigan, a leather belt with a bunch of keys swinging from her waist, an old apron, and heavy brogues over darned woollen stockings.[6] She prowled the grounds relentlessly, and not until he was in his hammock did a boy feel safe from her. Commander Gardner said of her that she had a habit of popping up anywhere and everywhere, always with some fault to find. Her outstanding characteristic, he felt, was an ability to discern moral turpitude in even minor faults. The assumption was that 'ordinary decent people always behaved in a way that was utterly honest and honourable. This meant that any boy whose behaviour fell below this artificial norm was rotten.'

Although the boys could tell something about Beatie's character and behaviour outside the House, they knew very little of her life inside it. A favoured few got as far as the pantry, and were responsible for carrying meals up from the galley, putting dishes on hot plates, then keeping out of the way until it was time to wash the dirty dishes and claim as their rightful 'perks' any food left over. Occasionally a member of staff lodged in the servants' quarters at the top of the House – perhaps a night officer who slept there during the day – but he had no part in the private life of those who lived there. He might witness curious events, but he would be unwise to discuss them outside. Gardner guessed at another world beyond the office, where the Frys lived 'the gracious life of country gentry'. It was a good guess, confirmed by the accounts of people who were the guests of C.B., cricketers and sports writers mainly, who enjoyed lavish dinners that seemed to take hours to consume. It is doubtful, however, if Beatie made more than a token appearance at meals, staying only as long as it took to eat and then getting back to work. She placed notebooks in all the places where boys cleaned, swept, scrubbed and polished, in which they reported on what they had done and – if they were in charge of a team – commented on the work of individuals. She read these every evening, adding her own terse comments on what she had seen during the day. The list of boys who had been to the lavatory was carefully examined. Only bowel movements were recorded: boys could urinate without supervision. If certain names – or rather numbers – did not appear regularly in this notebook, those concerned were not being 'regular' and were likely to get a dose of suitable 'opening' medicine. Visits to the heads were timed, and those who took more than five minutes had TLH –

'Too long at heads' – put against their numbers. This made her suspect the boys concerned were perched over their buckets for some more recondite pleasure, and their numbers went straight into the defaulters' list.

Whereas in most schools pupils take home reports intended for themselves and their parents to read, Beatie would publish her comments on boys in the ship's magazine which she edited. The magazine was for sale to parents who must have wondered at the extraordinary things she said about their sons. Sometimes she introduced the boys by their numbers, sometimes by name. In a 1928 edition she added their nicknames – 'the Owl', 'Hurricane Ned', 'Stonehenge' and 'the Gimlet'. Her remarks ranged from the waspish to the whimsical.

2127 Needs rhythm in his life and to love, keeping in touch with the sun and the moon and all big beautiful creations and going joyfully with these.[7]

2163 He must keep very young and learn to sing well songs that would charm fairies into listening.[8]

2187 A patient boy who needs masses of warm sunny air to close round him and make him feel how beautiful a wealth of beauty strewn indiscriminately for him can be, and to be content. He swims.[9]

2305 Indescribably idle.[10]

2417 He lacks any vestige of humility, a want which is so confusing as to make one mentally deficient.[11]

2463 He holds himself and his powers in very high esteem. As a talker he is a maniac.[12]

2480 His indolence is unplumbed.[13]

2496 . . . loves warmth, hates work, would live on a radiator.[14]

The worst she could do was to give no report at all, printing the boy's name and number with no comment whatsoever. One of the best, and a very rare one of its kind, read

2452 A thoroughly capable and efficient, non-talkative boy. What he sets out to
do he does well. He is thoroughly British. Twenty shillings to the pound.[15]

It would be interesting to discover what became of George Hannent,
whose report this was, and whose bearing and deeds won from
Beatie such fulsome praise.

If the magazines were revealing about the boys, they also revealed
quite a lot about the editor and her view of life. A footnote in
December 1921 reads 'Force, will, and love are the conquerors',[16]
while on the opposite page she says, 'Boxing we have done a great
deal more at with quite useful results. It is interesting to see boys
beaten but hanging on – it is good for them.'

Boxing took place on one night a week, and often included a
'punishment' fight in which two boys entered the ring grossly
mismatched. The one destined to lose had somehow offended the
authorities. There was no charge sheet, no appeal against the
sentence passed on him – that he should enter a boxing ring with
someone heavier, stronger and much more experienced than himself.
All the earlier bouts had been watched with enjoyment. Contestants
shook hands after the last bell and shrugged off bloody noses, cuts
and bruises. The punishment fight was watched in stony silence.

The bell went for the first round, and the battering began. With no
hesitation, without any prompting from the referee, whose
impartiality was now suspended, the stronger and more experienced
fighter tore into his opponent and hammered him round the ring.
Very soon the loser was covered in blood. The rounds were no longer
ruled by the clock. They continued until it was deemed that
sufficient injury had been done.

After that any trace of enjoyment of the evening vanished. There
remained the dry fear of wondering whose turn it would be next,
which of them, for reasons that were never explained, would end up
in the loser's corner. Two boys, perfectly good friends and with no
grudges, could be pitched against one another, and should the

stronger of the two fail to make a convincing show of beating the other senseless he would be back in the ring himself the following boxing night, this time matched with someone less charitably disposed. Beatie watched the worst bloodbath without a trace of dismay, and showed no pity for the most cruelly beaten loser. She would sit at the ringside shouting 'Make him bleed, boy! Make him bleed!'

In stark contrast, she could write in the magazine of her dismay at human weakness and man's inability to leave the earth and 'get up into the sky' – a feat she said she regularly achieved with the help of 'the right Pilot'. It was the practical mystic at work again, with a Cromwellian penchant for tough basic decisions made with the assurance of one who claimed to be in direct communication with God.

There was a wistful note in the magazine dated October 1926: 'Every one of our *Mercury* boys on joining the Royal Navy most surely is put on a useful job, but the news or the thanks never reaches us.'[17] It had simply not occurred to her that her struggle, whether for perfection in the boys or to keep viable the only organisation that gave her freedom and satisfaction, might not always be appreciated. 'Sharkey' Ward departed in December 1923, but it took a while for the shadow he cast to recede, and even when the number of boys who had passed through the ranks had reached 3500, only about 200 of them remained in regular touch with the ship by letter. A few more returned out of sheer curiosity to look with adult eyes, free at last from fear, on the place that had had such a profound effect on their lives. Beatie had done little to endear herself to them, being as harsh as any chief petty officer or the most hardened regimental sergeant major in the land. When boys arrived back at the beginning of term she had them paraded and looked them up and down with scorn for having grown their hair and 'gone soft' over the holidays. She treated them to a slightly polished version of the tirade they would get from the leaders of the lower deck – 'You horrible little boys!' replacing 'You 'orrible lot!' – and told them in no uncertain terms what she thought of them, that they would soon be back the way she wanted them, tough, fast, alert and utterly obedient. She reared over them, frightening them by her sheer size. Even in 1945 when age had reduced her physical stature so that she resembled, as a boy of that year put it, 'Grandma, in the cartoons by Giles', she still retained her awesome personality.

Captain R. E. Hutchins, who was second-in-command of Britain's last battleship, HMS *Vanguard*, and commander of the cruiser HMS *Tiger*, began his sea career on the *Mercury* in 1923, just in time to see the last of 'Sharkey' Ward. He was on board for five years, and witnessed a transition from a penal regime to something more acceptable to the world outside. He was three months short of his twelfth birthday when he arrived in Hamble. His brother who came with him was only eight. Their mother had died that year and their father, faced with the responsibility of bringing up seven sons, was glad to get two of them into boarding school.

Hutchins was never in any doubt that Beatie was the sole captain of the ship, with her daughters as able lieutenants. In his account of life on board he describes Beatie as 'deeply religious, kindly and strict'. He continues:

She personally organised the work of the school outside the classrooms, determining routines and writing out work lists in her bold hand. The standards demanded and achieved in dining hall and other buildings, including the chapel, were quite exceptional, and unequalled in anything I have met at sea or elsewhere.[18]

He was unimpressed with the academic standards. The curriculum was massively deficient in the subjects not immediately relevant to the business of turning boys into sailors. Thus his eight-year-old brother, unusually young to be at such a place, missed out on fundamental subjects such as English literature, history, geography and the sciences – subjects which older entrants would at least have had a smattering of before they joined, but would get no more of once through the gates on Satchell Lane.

Another result of this deficiency, though not touched on by Hutchins, was the crippling effect on boys who discovered that life at sea, when they encountered the real thing, was not for them. The gaps in their education left them so short of skills that might enable them to find alternative forms of employment that some stayed on in an occupation which they found disagreeable, but from which there seemed no escape.

In practical matters there were no deficiencies. Hutchins' own experience as a senior naval officer suggested that, apart from practical sea-going experience, standards on the *Mercury* were comparable to those required for petty officers. Divisional Officers in the Royal Navy entry establishments almost fought to get *Mercury* boys into their divisions when a new batch arrived, so useful were they in helping with the process of turning raw recruits into disciplined people like themselves.

That Captain Hutchins in retirement could speak of Beatie as a kindly woman gave another insight into her character. As time went on a few boys – Hutchins was the most notable – exhibited to such an outstanding extent the approved qualities of leadership, toughness and so forth that she softened, slightly at least, in their direction. They had become instruments of her rule, and left to their own devices they would exact the same high standards from those around them. In Hutchins' case high intelligence was added to all-round capability. In December 1927 he took nearly a quarter of the awards on Prize Day. HRH The Prince of Wales, who had been invited to hand out the prizes, suggested to him that he stay close at hand since Hutchins could barely get back to his seat before his name was called again.

If Hutchins represented the standards Beatie was striving to attain at the *Mercury*, the visit of the Prince of Wales represented a further stage in her rehabilitation into the society from which she had been excluded by the events of forty years earlier.

11 – 'Half Greek, half Malvolio!'

The 1920s were both the worst and the best years of Beatie's rule. In the early part of the decade her authority was so pitiless that half a century later men who had suffered it spoke of her as hard, mean, cruel, sadistic, unfeeling, unwomanly – one said that 'no *normal* woman could be so insensitive'. Such praise as she elicited was of the most grudging kind. She taught them sailing in cutters and whalers, and was clearly a better sailor than some of them would ever be. There were still tenders attached to the ship, such as the *Vishala*, a converted fishing craft, and Beatie would sometimes skipper one of these on a trip well out into the Solent. A favourite destination was Alum Bay on the Isle of Wight. If there was a good sea running many of the boys were seasick, but not Beatie. (Those who were not sick dined well, having commandeered the packed luncheons of those who were.) But the descriptions of her from the mid-1920s onwards are less bitter, though without exception her ability to strike fear into everybody is still mentioned with awe. By this time she seemed to have gained all the respect she was ever likely to require.

The trickle of ex-*Mercury* boys proceeding to commissions in the armed forces and the Merchant Navy – at least one rose to be Master of the *Queen Mary* – had become a flood, and even those who were not officer material invariably gave a good account of themselves. Many of them would undoubtedly have achieved high rank even without Beatie's so-called 'scientific system of character training', as advertised in a prospectus dated 1926. Most who went into the Royal Navy, however, acknowledged a debt to her for having set them on their careers with qualities of speed and resilience that placed them ahead of their competitors.

She had also achieved more than enough respectability. The visit by the Prince of Wales was followed two years later by one from the Duke of York, the Prince's brother and later King George VI. The official timetable for the visit ('11.30. His Royal Highness leaves Waterloo Station by train') was preceded by a list of those who held honorary offices in the governing body of the ship. It read:

President:

The Lord Bishop of Winchester

Vice-Presidents

Admiral C. S. Hickley, CB, MVO
The Rt Hon. The Earl of Birkenhead
Lord Apsley, DSO, MC
Lord Riddell
Montagu Rendall, Esq. LLD
Lord Louis Mountbatten
The Rt Hon. Lord Lee of Fareham, GCSI, etc.
Captain Basil Lubbock
The Rt Hon. Sir John Simon, KCVO, etc.
Professor Seward, SCD (Camb.), FRS
A. J. Spender, Esq.
Rear-Admiral C. Tibbitts, CBE, MVO, etc.
H. E. The Hon. Sir F. Stanley Jackson
The Hon. Mr Justice Roache
Rear-Admiral B. G. Thesiger, CB, etc.[1]

Undoubtedly C.B.'s friendship with these men, some of whom he knew from Oxford or the cricket field, served to bring them together, but it was not enough to explain so much greatness, so many accomplished figures, ready to associate themselves with a tiny nautical school in Hampshire. Half of their number would have looked well on the headed notepaper of the richest public schools. It had to be that Beatie had made the *Mercury* the best in its class, that of privately-owned nautical schools. If it was the best in England, then it was one of the best in the world, and the great men's names added still further distinction.

There was, however, just the vaguest suspicion that people were still shy of being associated too closely with Beatie. In January 1979 Admiral of the Fleet the Earl Mountbatten of Burma, writing of his link with the ship when he was its president in its closing years, long after Beatie and C.B. had gone, remarked, 'We all heard stories about how she [Beatie] ran the *Mercury* on a very taut discipline and she was respected, but also feared.'[2] What Mountbatten did not mention was that his connection pre-dated his presidency by many years, that he had been a vice-president in the 1920s, and he had not just 'heard stories'. Only after his tragic death in 1979 did this come to light, with evidence that he and his wife had often visited the ship when Beatie was running it. Nor had events surrounding the origins of the *Mercury* been forgotten even in the 1930s. Professor Sir Geoffrey Callender of the Royal Naval College, Greenwich, wrote to Sir James Caird in February 1930, on the subject of Charles Hoare's collection of ship models and naval artefacts which Sir James had acquired for the maritime museum in Greenwich. Callender spoke in his letter of a visit to the college by 'our friend Schweder [who] brought with him [Lord] Arthur Somerset':

I showed the two of them the Mercury models and other treasures. Somerset, who is a man of seventy-four, knew Hoare very well and filled up several gaps in our knowledge of his career. Somerset said that the lady [Beatie] broke her leg in the hunting field when Hoare was Master of the Vale of White Horse, [and] stayed in Hoare's house so long that two things happened; one, Mrs Hoare left her husband, and two, the surrounding country declined to allow Hoare to draw their coverts. He was in consequence compelled to give up the pack, and it was then that he took up the Training Ship Mercury. Somerset also added that Hoare and the lady had several children, but here the chronicle becomes almost too scandalous to put on paper . . . Poor Beatrice.[3]

Although Lord Somerset was mistaken in some of his details – Beatie did not break her leg, nor did Mrs Hoare leave her husband altogether until four years after the 'accident' in the hunting field – it is clear that the Gloucestershire scandal was remembered and discussed, and not with any particular affection.

The 1920s gave way to the 1930s with Beatie still in command, and her daughters still assisting her. The new decade began with a new building, the recreation hall having been destroyed by fire. The brick structure that went up in its stead was subsequently referred to as the 'New Place' and had a figure of the god Mercury poised on the roof. Inside were panelled walls and murals painted by Gregory Robinson.

For the remaining years of Beatie's life only minor changes took place in the daily routine. Some of the more futile punishments disappeared as the men who had devised them reached retirement. The floggings ceased after a boy emerged from one with blood running down the backs of his legs – and ran home on the same day. In the dining hall wooden bowls and spoons had given way to normal dishes and cutlery – a mixed blessing to the boys, one of whose duties was to clean and polish every item as if their lives depended on it.

Throughout the 1920s and 1930s C. B. Fry was absent for long spells, but though his appearances on the site at Hamble were brief, the impression he made was never less than striking. Walker, who was comforted by him when life was becoming unbearable, tells of his arriving on the playing field unexpectedly when boys were playing cricket.

He took the bat from one of the boys and showed how it should be held. Then he gave us a display of his agility. He sent a boy to get a chair. When it was fetched Cdr. Fry stood behind it, his feet flexed.

'Now you should all be able to do this,' he said to the little crowd that had collected.

He suddenly went down so that he was nearly sitting on his heels. Then he shot up into the air and landed in front of the chair, bolt upright and with both feet still together. It was a marvellous display of agility – and showmanship.[4]

C.B. was then forty-eight. In his mid-fifties he was demonstrating athletics, 'floating over the hurdles', as one witness put it, and ten years later he was seen by Andrew McGavin, a son of the ship's bandmaster, diving off the main deck of the dormitory ship into the narrow gap between the landing stage and the moored cutters, and surfacing yards away on the other side of them.

Mobsby – he who had taken a sixpence or two off C.B. in the nets – described him at one of his more relaxed pastimes:

Any boy who had business in the field in the early morning would often see C.B. in pyjamas and ornate dressing gown, sitting on one of the wooden seats which surrounded the ground, fishing rod in hand, casting a fly on to a postcard lying on the grass about twenty to thirty feet away.[5]

This was the picture presented by all accounts of C.B. enjoying himself on the ship: eccentric – what normal commanding officer would be caught practising fly-fishing in his pyjamas? – and showing off a little, but generally detached from the day-to-day slog of the place. E. W. Swanton remarked in his book, *Sort of a Cricketing Person*, that 'Nothing was undersize about Charles [Fry]',[6] and added, 'least of all his kindness to the young'. It was an aspect of his character he seldom showed in a place dedicated to spartan living, but at least his presence was unmenacing and his image as a noble man unspoilt. On the rare occasion when he interfered in the running of the ship it was still in keeping with his image. When he saw a boy being bullied, he took him aside and arranged for him to have an intensive course in boxing. It was not a 'Sharkey' Ward course. He was taught to duck, weave, think fast, and hit without getting hit too often in return. Satisfied that the difference in the abilities between bullied and bully had been narrowed, he put them in the ring together and saw his protégé turn the tables so effectively that the loser started to fight foul, kicking and hitting below the belt. C.B. had a riding crop handy and beat him soundly, probably the only occasion he ever struck a boy, but one which was unmistakably just.

In the village of Hamble the same impression prevailed – of a man who was pleasantly eccentric, kind, but rather remote, too taken up with his affairs in places as far afield as London, Geneva and India to have time to concern himself with local matters.

The busy life elsewhere was perhaps too busy. The League of Nations met in Geneva in 1920 with C.B. as an acting substitute Delegate of the Indian representation, writing speeches for K. S. Ranjitsinhji. Back in England the following year, he made the first of three unsuccessful attempts to get into Parliament, standing for the Liberals at Brighton. The same year, he travelled to India in time for the 1921–2 visit by the Prince of Wales. A year later it was politics again, fighting Banbury for the Liberals. Back at the League of Nations in 1923, he wrote the speech delivered by Ranjitsinhji which probably checked Mussolini's ambitions in the Adriatic after he had sent ships to bombard and occupy Corfu. While still at Geneva there occurred that strange episode when a bishop from Albania was authorised to find 'an English country gentleman with ten thousand a year' to become King of Albania, the throne being vacant. Ranjitsinhji handled the negotiations; C.B. was actually interviewed by the bishop, but nothing came of it. (To *Mercury* boys, had they heard of this, the prospect of C.B. as king of that country would have been less intriguing than that of his wife as his Queen and Consort, and the effect this might have on the Albanians.)

C.B. made his third and final attempt to gain a seat in Parliament in 1924, when he stood at Oxford. His defeat did not mean the end of his busy life outside the *Mercury*, however. His acquaintance with powerful, wealthy and talented people took him to all parts of the country and to India.

Whether it was the furious pace of his life or some incident in the course of a visit to India which brought on the bout of mental illness that overwhelmed C.B. for several years is impossible to decide with any accuracy. His behaviour was bizarre – he was said to have run naked along Brighton beach, and at home he hugged his possessions in fear of their being stolen by imaginary thieves. For the first few years of the 1930s he had to be looked after by a nurse, often staying at a house in Maidenhead made available to him by Ranjitsinhji. Ironically, C.B. could not bear to see his benefactor, as a curious manifestation of his illness was a horror of Indians. There were times when he was lucid and in possession of all his faculties, and then he would be taken to visit the homes of sympathetic friends. He could discuss his symptoms with them. The Begbie family, at whose house he was always welcome, listened to him as he described his feelings when emerging from a passage of the illness in its most extreme form. For a while as he surfaced he was apparently beyond com-munication, neither responding to the people about him nor offering any sign of what he was feeling or thinking, but he assured the Begbies that he was fully aware of what was happening. He told them how he had been to a house for tea, the chauffeur, who also acted as a nurse, taking him in the Bentley. His host poured boiling water into the teapot without first putting in the tea leaves. C.B. saw the error and did nothing, then watched the confusion, still without comment or the slightest reaction, as clear water was poured into the cups.

During one of his lucid spells he was invited to a house in the New Forest to meet the Headmaster of Picket Post School, Frank Andrews. Like C.B., Andrews had graduated in classics at Oxford, and the two men sat at opposite ends of a first-floor balcony overlooking the forest and declaimed Greek verse to each other. Joan Begbie was there at the time, and, for her, the huge delight C.B. showed on this occasion was a clue to his condition. As the evening wore on he shed his years and the burden of his illness and became young and vital again, the Greek god of Wadham, at one with the heroes in the verses he shouted into the night. For years his life had swung between the poles of a frantic public life and the rigidly governed affairs of the *Mercury*, affairs in which he had very little say. At neither pole did he find a response as refreshing as that to be had from a former classics scholar like himself.

When Beatie was asked what had brought on her husband's illness she replied 'thwarted genius'.[7] It was a revealing reply; it told the questioner as much about Beatie as it did about her husband. She treated him with compassion throughout the whole period of his illness, and there is little to suggest that the domineering manner, which characterised her dealings with the boys on the ship, had helped to bring it about; but her own lack of education, her inability to respond to her husband in an area and on a theme which was crucial to his life, may have been a contributory factor.

The illness receded in 1934, and C.B. attended his only son's wedding to Yvonne Blunt of New Jersey. The caption to a newspaper photograph, taken outside a London registry office, read, 'Mr Fry (C.B.) who is 62, has, to the great joy of his army of friends, made a complete recovery after a serious health breakdown.'[8]

There were five more years in the public eye before C.B. slipped into the shadows, with only one or two glimpses thereafter before his death in 1956. He travelled to Germany in 1934 to meet the leaders of the Nazi Party, Baldur von Schirach, Rust, Minister of Culture, Hess, Ribbentrop and Hitler. In England he continued his work as a sports correspondent, and in this capacity left for a round-the-world tour late in 1936 in the company of Neville Cardus, who was sure that, if he had put his mind to it, C.B. could have won the highest honours in half a dozen lofty walks of life. 'He walked the field half Greek, half Malvolio,' was another phrase Cardus used to describe him, invoking at once the fickle gods of ancient legend and the giddy poseur of *Twelfth Night* in an attempt to pin down the elusive qualities of this strange man. Writing of their voyage together, Cardus told how C.B. held court amongst the deck-chairs on the *Orion* as she ploughed patiently through the seas:

He dressed differently every day; sometimes with topee and short leather trousers, as though about to trace the source of the Amazon; or in a scaled green sort of costume which made him look like a deep-sea monster; or in a bath towel, worn like a toga. One day, to tease him, I said, 'Good morning, Charles. No hemlock yet? Give us your ideas about the Iambic.' In full spate came forth a swift survey of the origin and development of the Iambic, with quotations from all periods and writers, every sentence ending with 'You see what I mean' or 'However'. A sort of intellectual Jack Bunsby; an original and fascinating man. Even Hitler heard of him and invited him to Berlin to consult him on the right way of physical training amongst Die Jugend.[9]

It was inevitable that a man of such extraordinary character and intellect, with such a varied career to look back on, and a considerable flair for words, should write his autobiography. It was published in October 1939, much of it having been dictated to his friend, Denzil Batchelor. In his own book about C.B., Batchelor records his amazement at the ease with which the lines were delivered, page after page filling up with rarely a pause for alterations. All the sport was there, the cricket, the athletics, rugger and soccer – his joy in the latter sometimes showing through even more than in his first love, cricket. Every chapter glittered with famous names, so many that they make up the greater part of a nine-page closely printed index – sportsmen, scholars, writers, artists, princes and maharajahs, earls and actresses, all of them met on equal terms, and attracting the same kind of lively anecdotes.

A whole chapter was devoted to the visit to Germany and his encounter with Hitler. He did not, in fact, go there so that Hitler could consult him about the type of physical training most appropriate to Die Jugend. A possible rapprochement between the German youth movement and whatever might be its opposite number in England provided the rationale for the invitation to C.B. to meet the Nazi leaders in Berlin and at the Brown House in Munich. C.B.'s brief was to explain to them that things were run on slightly untidy and far more liberal lines in England, but he was subjected to the most persuasive propaganda, treated to images of a disciplined people, an immense concourse of land-workers assembling outside Munich, there to be harangued by Hitler. C.B. wrote:

There was no question that the people were devoted to the Fuehrer, and there was no question that the world of fields and valleys round Munich was a world of work, simple-minded and disciplined. I cannot refrain from saying that the atmosphere of effective discipline strongly appealed to me.[10]

From a man whose life had been devoted almost entirely to his own pleasure, even though he had in turn given pleasure to countless others, it was an unfortunate admission. While tactfully explaining to the Nazis that their youth movement could find no counterpart in England, he nevertheless seemed to wish that there was such an institution in his native land and that the English workers would march for their leaders in the same way that the German land-workers marched for the Fuehrer, 'their spades and forks and hoes at the slope after the manner of soldiers'.[11]

From Munich C.B. returned to Berlin and a meeting with Hitler. No doubt the Nazi leader had been primed with information about the man he was to meet, and knew that C.B. was on familiar terms with the highest in his own country and further afield, bearing in mind his association with the League of Nations. What passed between them would most certainly echo through the corridors of power in London and perhaps find space in the London newspapers.

The meeting was staged to make the maximum impact on the visitor, with the two men seeing each other for the first time from opposite ends of a long room in the Reich Chancellery. They saluted each other, and marched towards the centre, Hitler keeping in step with his visitor. Ribbentrop introduced them and acted as interpreter. What followed was less a conversation than a persuasive monologue on the part of Hitler in which he outlined his nation's problems, the need to re-arm, the threat of Communism, the menace of the Jews who had, he said, 'obtained a stranglehold on finance, medicine, law, and all the learned professions'.[12] There was mention of the youth movement, but no advice from C.B. as to how it should be trained.

They talked for an hour and a quarter. There was a repeat performance of the theatrical opening to the meeting, only in reverse order, Hitler timing his arrival at his desk so that he turned at the same instant as his visitor. They saluted each other, and C.B.'s last image was of the Fuehrer back behind his desk, head down, working steadily.

Writing in 1939, five years after the meeting, C.B. found no reason to change his view of Hitler and Germany as he had found them. He was impressed by what he had seen and heard – as a great many other English visitors had been – and said so. It may be that he had seen in Germany on a large scale an equivalent to the life created by Beatie at the *Mercury*, tidy, organised, ruthless, efficient, all emotion channelled, all energies directed towards a few simple goals, with no messy asides and little room for imagination.

A chapter is devoted by C.B. to the *Mercury*. It consists of a quick gallop through the history of the ship from its foundation by Charles Hoare in 1885, but contains no reference to the background to the event. On minor details there are mistakes. The old sailing ship is incorrectly spelled *Illova*. There is the fanciful account of her career 'searching for wind in the China Seas'. Hoare's collection of ship models is valued at 'less than £3000 at probate', when in fact the sum was £5737. Much of C.B.'s time is seen to have been taken up with organising the ship's finances, getting subscriptions from friends to back his application to the High Court for the *Mercury* to be established as an educational charity and thus ensure its continued existence, and thereafter keeping the place solvent by astute management of funds and sharing a host of duties with his wife in order to cut down on expenditure. He negotiates the sale of the model ships to the National Maritime Museum, after Sir Geoffrey Callender, Greg Robinson and others had revealed their true worth. The small print in Hoare's will is not revealed, nor is there any indication of the true state of affairs whereby C.B. made it possible for the place to survive after he had, as one of his bandmasters put it, 'cast the mantle of his fame about the ship' – and then left the entire day-to-day running of it to his wife, Sybil and Charis. Beatie is acclaimed as a 'genius in all that concerns routine work and domestic economy', while he is employed mainly in the organisation of the instructional side and what are loosely called 'foreign relations'. He goes on, 'The *Mercury* is the only example I know of two captains of a ship with a successful result. Although I am nominally the head of the establishment, my wife and I have always acted as two persons in one – like the consuls at Rome.'[13]

They may indeed have run the ship on these lines, with C.B. an equal force but not considering it necessary to appear as such. However, since so much that went on was so completely uncharacteristic of the man the belief was reinforced that he had little to do with it. He was conspicuously kind and fair in his few direct dealings with the boys, and it was hard to believe that he approved of some of the more outrageous punishments that took place. Nor did observers fail to notice that when royalty appeared on the premises, or any important visitor came to inspect them, it was Beatie who took charge, with her husband several paces behind, playing prince consort to her queen. And it was Beatie who got the OBE.

C.B.'s cursory account of his role on the *Mercury* is introduced by an anecdote concerning Lord Birkenhead. Visiting his friend, and standing in the rose garden overlooking the Hamble, said 'This is a lovely place and a fine show, C.B., but for you it has been a backwater.'[14]

The episode echoed another story about both men: that in their Oxford days C.B. joined the cricket club and went on to make runs, while Lord Birkenhead, F. E. Smith as he was then, joined the Oxford Union – and went on to make history.

12 – Reaching Home

The war years, 1939–45, were the last in which the *Mercury* management could fairly claim that their system of training was suited to the demands of the Royal Navy. The business of the *Mercury* was war, and such refinements as a library or a science lab did not exist in a place devoted quite properly, as they felt, to producing the kind of recruits the Navy wanted. On Prize Day there were nine prizes for school subjects, including Divinity, Reading and Recitation, but there were the same number of prizes awarded for 'Qualities', such as 'Initiative', 'Cheerful Obedience', 'Perseverance', and 'Unselfishness and Good Humour', all of which reinforced the quality that lay at the heart of their training – the ability to offer blind obedience to whoever was in charge, and, in time, to move up the ladder of authority and expect the same attitudes from those below them. They were highly disciplined, these *Mercury* boys: but in 1945 a handful of men had flown in comfort and without much hazard to themselves to the skies over Hiroshima and Nagasaki and blasted both cities flat, and in a few seconds had called into question the concept of discipline as it was understood on the *Mercury*. The great navies of the world had been rendered obsolete at a stroke, and new forms of excellence, new disciplines, were suddenly in demand that had nothing to do with the Edwardian virtues of 'Cheerful Obedience' and 'Unselfishness and Good Humour'. In the Building the boys were tutored in choral speech, and dutifully recited,

> Canst follow the track of the Dolphin
> Or tell where the sea swallows roam?

Where Leviathan taketh his pastime,
What oceans he calleth his home?

Even so with the words of the rulers,
And the orders those words shall convey,
There is no other law besides this one:
Thou shalt not criticise, but obey![1]

Suddenly, the uncritical recruit had become a liability in a world in which sophisticated weaponry demanded technological and mathematical skills. The more highly-trained ratings would be unlikely to accord unquestioning obedience to the old-fashioned type of petty-officer, whose only claim to respect was his ability to terrorise people. The radar technician thus terrorised would quietly take his precious skills elsewhere.

If the rank-and-file of the *Mercury* could not recognise these changes, it was to be hoped that their immediate superiors could: but their precarious tenure, holding office only as long as they too gave blind obedience to the woman in charge, ruled out the possibility of change, while she, for her part, showed no sign of losing her grip on the place. Week after week they saw her appear, moving slowly, as became her eighty-three years, but sturdily. If they sought signs of weakening powers in her voice or expression there were none to record. Sybil was her eyes and ears in the places she could not reach on her own, and her rule was absolute. Her son and her daughters by C. B. Fry had long since left, the daughters to join the WRNS where, by this time, they had become Chief Officers, the equivalent of Commanders in the RN; but their departure had altered nothing.

How long could this last? At some point Beatie had to be told that she had gone on too long. Or would the end come in another way, from the reluctance of parents to send their sons to a school so obviously out of touch with the times? Already there was a suspicion that people in local governments up and down the country with scholarships to dispense were sending 'problem' boys who were 'in need of discipline' to the ship. There were boys from preparatory schools in the ranks, one at least of whom had been misled into thinking that he was going to attend 'the Eton of the south', and though they were in the minority, they represented the type of youth that had been the backbone of the place for years, sons of people who set a high value on the boarding school that offered a rugged outdoor life as part of the educational experience, and also one that, for all the deficiencies of its curriculum, still carried the aura of C. B. Fry. Such boys now found that they had strange companions, like the one who at first amused his Watch by stealing all the bootlaces of a neighbouring Watch, and then shocked them by stealing all theirs as well. He went on to loot their hiding places of stamps, envelopes, writing paper and money, the very things they had stored away in defiance of all attempts to stop them getting letters through to the outside world. Not even being flung into the mud of the Hamble at low tide checked him; it seemed that he was not alone, that there were others like him scattered through the sections, boys of a type who had not been welcome even in the days when Charles Hoare was looking for recruits in Shoreditch and Hackney Wick.

I was one of those who expected the *Mercury* to be a rather more glamorous kind of public school. I write of the final years of Beatie's rule with the vivid recollection of a personal traumatic experience.

In the autumn of 1945, an evening of boxing came to an end with Boy No. 3488 Crabtree cast as executioner in a punishment fight. When the bell went for the first round, Crabtree dutifully tore into his opponent in full knowledge that there was at least one beefy oaf at the ringside who would do the same to him a week later if he hesitated. In no time at all he reduced his opponent to a bloody shambles. The obsession with cleanliness on the *Mercury* did not extend to the canvas on which they fought. It was brown with the spilt blood of hundreds of fights, and now it was showered with more bright specks which would dry and blend with the rest. A right from Crabtree, and his opponent's head snapped back, and the scarlet spray scattered as far as the benches lining the ringside. The first round went on too long, and the contestants had barely sat down when the bell went for the second. Crabtree came forward, punched hard, and then held back as fresh blood ran from the other boy's face. For a few moments they prodded each other, the predictable winner feeling he had done enough damage for one evening, and the loser relieved that the barrage of hard blows had ceased. Suddenly there was a roar from the ringside. The duty officer was half way to his feet and shouting in frightened rage: 'Get in there and beat him! If you don't I'll come in and beat both of you myself!'

Crabtree resumed the punishment, but the instigator of this fight was sitting in her living-room on the first floor of the House, poring over the details of the work done that day and preparing for the next. With only a few months to live, she seemed unaware of any alternative to setting men and boys at each other's throats, demanding, bullying, driving, never letting up in the pursuit of what she saw as her duty. And there was no alternative while individuals and nations felt compelled to compete rather than to co-operate. She seemed to personify not only the waste of women's capabilities, but those of all humanity.

The winter of 1945–6 was cold and wet. There were gales strong enough to stop the movement of shipping in the Solent, but on the Hamble the traffic of boats between the pier and the dormitory ship went on uninterrupted. One January morning the rough weather crew, having put the ship's company ashore, became too exhausted to return the cutter to its moorings, and were swept up river. They landed at Bursledon, and early risers were treated to the spectacle of eleven boys in oilskins, barefooted, padding silently along the pavements in the direction of Hamble village.

The Easter holidays in April were approaching when Andrew's brother, Eric McGavin, sent Beatie details of a mid-week concert. She had a high regard for him as a son of the first bandmaster, James McGavin, the man who had coaxed great music out of the boys for half a century, and who had once put on a complete performance of

Wagner's *Parsifal*. She sent Eric terse little notes about the running of the ship, scribbled on anything that came to hand, an old bill or the back of an envelope. One of these read: 'I missed the Band this morning. Was there any reason for the Band not playing? The boys need very firm treatment at the moment. As far as I am concerned they shall have it.'[2] However, in her comments approving his programme for the Wednesday concert, Beatie appended an un-characteristic statement – one that hinted at some self-questioning and suggested that she had a presentiment of her impending death.

Two days previously, at Saturday Divisions, she had stopped in the middle of her inspection and, for the first time in the memory of most of those present, addressed the whole gathering: 'I wish you would not call each other by your numbers. I wish you would call each other by your names. Numbers are so insensitive.' Six days later she fell and broke her hip. She stayed in her own bedroom for three days, during which time all bugle calls ceased, and orders were given softly so that she might not be disturbed. Boots, which in any case were worn only for drill, were left in their lockers. On 15 April she was taken to the RHS Infirmary, Southampton, where little Geoffrey Petch had stopped on his way home to a grave on the banks of the Humber.

It was Wednesday of that week when McGavin assembled the ship's company in the chapel. He bade us kneel and bow our heads. There was a long pause before he could bring himself to speak. He was a tall man, with the erect carriage of one who had been in the band of the Grenadier Guards. He was handsome, with strong black hair swept back from a pale, lean, slightly ascetic face. I looked up and saw that this face was full of anguish, and that he was close to tears. At last he began, 'The time has come to tell you that there is no hope for Mrs Fry.' He went on to tell of a life of dedication, over half a century devoted utterly to the establishment of which we were a part. He did not reveal the extraordinary circumstances that had set her on this course. Perhaps he did not know of them.

We left the ship for the Easter holidays, and returned a fortnight later to learn that Beatie had reached Home on 23 April, and had been cremated. In her will she asked – enigmatically – for her ashes to 'be scattered in the air'. In fact they were scattered on the rose gardens which she had planted overlooking the Hamble River.

A few weeks later, the priest who had given her the last rites of the Church was officiating at a communion service in the chapel, attended by a few boys who came to the altar rail to receive the bread and wine. One of them asked afterwards why communion had not been given to the old lady kneeling beside him. He had been next to the place where Beatie had always knelt.

No tears were shed for Beatie, at least not among the boys she had ruled. The local newspaper assured its readers – in case there should have been any doubt – that the *Mercury* boys had loved her.[3] A few may have felt that way – the sons of James McGavin, perhaps, who had grown up in the shadow of the *Mercury*, had trained there, and had then returned as adults with privileged access to the House, and so to another side of Beatie's character. The rest regarded her with awe, pity, admiration, loathing, fear, respect – a whole range of emotions – but certainly not love. Boys had always been known to her by their numbers, even the few to whom she had given nicknames, and it was difficult to feel love for a person who ruled your life with a rod of iron, and treated you as a cypher. Too late she had appealed to us to use each other's names, and told us what we already knew, that numbers were 'insensitive'.

The new term began with a whiff of change. Would Sybil Hoare assume the role of her mother and inspect us on Saturday mornings? She did not, but continued examining our work, the cleaning, polishing, and scrubbing we had done, while Fraser conducted the ceremonies at the Verandah exactly as if Beatie had been there.

The only dramatic change was in Miss Hoare's appearance. She was dressed from head to toe in new clothes; her hair, which had always been pulled back and tied up in a bun, was more informally arranged, and one could see that it had a natural curl. She seemed more approachable, and even attempted a smile and a few pleasantries in her dealings with us. Lacking any insight into the nature of her relationship with her mother, we saw this as an indication that she was celebrating her release from decades of subservience. Equally celebratory, perhaps, was the bonfire Sybil made of the mass of papers and photographs that had been cleared out of her mother's rooms. Documents invaluable to future biographers and historians went up in smoke, destroyed by the living who wished to close doors on the past. In this case, however, it is very likely that the dead also wanted the past forgotten. Beatie, aware that her life had run on more than ordinary lines, indicated to one of her staff, a man who had worked for her for many years, that she did not want her story told. Loyal servant that he was, he kept her secrets, and turned away many who came to him for help, believing, quite rightly, that there was a gripping tale to be told about how a woman came to be in charge of a nautical school for boys, but unable to get at the roots of the story. He may, in fact, have known very little about her, no more perhaps than the garbled account given by Lord Arthur Somerset to Sir Geoffrey Callender, but even this he kept to himself in loyalty to Beatie.

A month after Beatie's death a memorial service was held for her in the ship's chapel, attended by high ranking officers of the armed forces including Admiral of the Fleet Sir James Somerville. The officiating priest was the Revd A. L. E. Hoskyns-Abrahall, a former naval officer and a future bishop. He described her as a genius, but added that her genius was not some gift that made it easier for her to do her work than other people. 'It was rather,' he went on, 'that classical definition of genius, an infinite capacity for taking pains.' No doubt he thought he had paid further tribute to her when he remarked that 'She went on where lesser men would have stopped satisfied.'[4]

It was a sentence which unwittingly embraced the whole triumph and tragedy of her life. If a man had achieved as much there would have been no memorial service, no gathering of admirals and other officers to honour his memory, since he would have achieved no more than was expected of him. But a woman had done this, and, while it was unquestionably a triumph for her, it was also a tragedy, for, if the assembly had thought about it at all, they would have found it monstrous that there were regiments of women, armies of them, perhaps, with as much courage, staying power and fortitude, and certainly with far greater intellects than the woman they were honouring, yet with little or no recognition of their powers, singly or collectively, nor adequate space in which to exercise them. The constraints of her early life had left her with only her strength of character as the means to success, which may have explained why so many of the prizes awarded on the ship each year went to boys who displayed similar qualities. She was accustomed to say that inspiration was better than information. For the uninformed this might be sufficient, but the discriminating prefer an inspired performance from actors who know their lines.

In the *Mercury Magazine* of March 1927, a footnote reads, 'A great ship asks deep waters.'[5] Beatrice Holme Fry was like a great ship, rammed hard aground in the shallows of the Hamble. Nevertheless, she fought for over half a century to make, then to keep, a foothold in the world worthy of her extraordinary talent, that of moulding the lives of others to her own standards. Those standards were high, and it was her fate that she should work among men and in that hitherto most manly of occupations, seafaring. Generations of *Mercury* boys paid dearly in order that Beatie might succeed against all the odds, but at least they entered the services so highly trained that most won immediate advancement. No one could be allowed to think for a moment that a woman would demand less of those around her than a man would, and so the rules became stricter and the expectations higher than they had been under Charles Hoare. It was no surprise to anyone on the premises that all hands could be mustered for inspection by Winston Churchill in less than ten minutes. The place was always ready for inspection, but the visitor did not get to see the effort required to maintain this level of preparedness. They did not see Reid's brutal game of 'luffs and tackles', the dreary file of barefoot boys jogging by the hour round the signal mast, the occasional figure shivering for hours at the cross-trees of the same mast, the terrified boy tied hand and foot to the gun for a flogging, the crumpled figure on the grass of the sports field when a 'shake-up' had gone on too long.

For all that she had fought so long and hard, it is not enough to ascribe her tough stance to the need to succeed in a man's world. There was the struggle – successful as it turned out – for recognition by the aristocracy who had excluded her in the aftermath of the Gloucestershire Scandal. Recognition, however, could not bring back the grandeur of life at Hatchlands, something she may have hoped to recover in her initial and childish infatuation for a rich man, and subsequently in an almost grim attachment to him that went on even after his death, attending his grave and keeping his seat in the chapel decorated with flowers. She was like Tennyson's 'great Princess' – 'grand, epic, homicidal' – but in the end she could find no larger estate in which to be her regal self than the forty-five acres sandwiched between Satchell Lane and the river. Some saw her life at the *Mercury* as a long expiation for a decade of youthful folly, and the intense nature of her religious life as an element in this. There was no denying her devotion to the ideal of the crucified Christ, 'The Green Hill King', as she called Him. At almost every Prize Day concert in the Building the Prelude to *Parsifal* was played; the programme notes included the words 'Only through pain and suffering can peace be won';[6] and in a letter to Eric McGavin she wrote, 'We need to remember we have to go up the hill ourselves to the Cross.'[7] She was ready to accept hardship, and she imposed it in cruel measure on those under her command.

Only when death was a few days away did she seem to acknowledge at last that there was an alternative; the way of love. In her letter to Eric, having approved his programme for the mid-week concert, she said, 'I think amongst my thoughts much about Death, Silence, Quiet Spirits, so wonderful – and the Love that has been spent for us all regardless of what we are.' Quite how she could have reconciled the Christian doctrine of love with the harsh necessities of life for a woman running an all-male establishment must remain a dilemma of universal concern, one that makes her life – in the fullest classical sense – a profound tragedy.

Epilogue

If Beatie was a 'genius' to the extent of possessing an infinite capacity for taking pains, her husband was one on a more generous scale. 'The true genius,' wrote Samuel Johnson, 'is a mind of large general powers accidentally determined to some particular direction.'[1] That C.B. had such powers was universally recognised. When advancing years inevitably diminished his prowess at sport, one might have expected that his intellectual gifts would have given him the power to develop a different, but equally eminent, career. Based on the *Mercury*, whether from a sense of duty or from an inability to organise his powers to more purpose, he fell short of his countrymen's expectations. The forays to India and to the League of Nations were no substitute for the achievements expected of a man who had shown promise of becoming one of 'the choice and master spirits of this age', and Neville Cardus's description of him as 'the admirable Crichton of games' put the seal on a career over which must hang more darkly than for most the shadow of what might have been. C.B. may have known this. In 1946, I came ashore at dawn before the rest of the company and saw the old man dressed in a greatcoat, staring across the river at the dormitory ship, with a look on his face of one who had stumbled on Dresden minutes after the bombers had left.

After his wife's death in 1946, C. B. Fry struggled briefly to keep the *Mercury* unchanged. Beatie had possessed a charismatic power which had held the system whole, bound in a strong chain. When it snapped things fell apart, and no one was on the scene with her authority to weld them together again. The charismatics are undemocratic. They do not confer freedoms on the people who come into their shadow. Those in the shadow may prefer it that way, finding ease from the burden of decisions.

In 1950 C.B. retired to a flat in Andover Court, a block of flats on the corner of Hendon Way and the Finchley Road in north-west London. Stephen and Yvonne Fry took over a hotel, The Master Builder, on the banks of the Beaulieu River. Sybil Hoare went with them. (There is a little chapel in the grounds of the hotel which contains a kneeler Beatie used in the *Mercury* chapel. It is embroidered with her initials.) C.B. visited his family at Beaulieu, and residents of the hotel found little mementoes of his life as sportsman scattered through the building – photographs on the walls, or his old cricket bag left casually on a landing as though he were still about to carry it purposefully into a pavilion. In truth C.B. had become almost a recluse, spending most of his time in London.

There was a brief return to the limelight in 1955 when he was guest of honour on the television programme, *This Is Your Life*. The carefully staged pleasantries, the figures from the great man's past previously drilled in what to say, filled out the usual half hour of television time with the details of an astonishing career. There seemed to be no shadows, no dark corners, to mar the impression that this had indeed been a life worth living.

After C.B.'s death the following year many of his own generation, and the hero-worshipping generation that came after, expressed their regrets that the promise of his early days had not been fulfilled. His box at Lords in 1912 had overflowed with men who had come to honour him, Chesterton, Belloc, E. V. Lucas, John Drinkwater, Rider Haggard, Clifford and Arnold Bax – men whose works endure where his are barely remembered. In the lives and the autobiographies of the great, the famous and the powerful who dined at his table in the House at Hamble – Churchill, Baden-Powell, Kipling and many others – there is little or no mention of their meetings with C.B. When he does come to their notice he is hedged about with reservations. Sir Maurice Bowra, Warden of Wadham College from

1938 to 1970, described him as 'eager and natural ... though perhaps he lived on a manic curve, of which I never saw the downward trend',[2] while Lord Birkenhead, the second Earl, said of C.B. that the brilliant early promise petered out in after years 'into a somewhat desultory and disappointed career'.[3] That C.B. in his declining years at the *Mercury* should lie awake at nights reciting aloud the details of the games he had played was a source of dismay to some who knew of this habit. The charitable said it was the sports writer in him recalling the game in order that he might write about it the following day for his newspaper column, but others were saddened that so much greatness had come to this – reliving former glories in the absence of present acclaim. Had he stayed on at Oxford, he could have been the glory of his university, classics don, writer and sportsman, in life a glittering presence at the college of his choice, in death a legend that would have grown with every new telling. But he stepped instead into the path of one of the most dynamic women of his generation.

C.B. died in London on 7 September 1956, aged eighty-four. He had had a long innings, but not the great one forecast for him when he went out to bat. He was cremated and his ashes taken not to the *Mercury* and the rose gardens, nor to any family resting place, but to Repton, there to be buried in the shadow of the parish church, with its slim elegant spire, and a few yards from the boundary of the school where he may have known the only true happiness in his long and varied career.

The departure of C. B. Fry and Sybil Hoare from the *Mercury* in 1950 had marked the end of an era. Many changes had to be made, beginning with the items of routine which owed more to the whims of the departing management than to established naval practice. An end was made to the weirder aspects of Saturday morning inspections, less emphasis was placed on the religious life, and the routine on the dormitory ship was completely overhauled. No longer would a lonely walker on Satchell Lane hear, in the late evening, the ethereal sound of a choir of 150 voices singing an evening hymn through the open gunports. And never again would a duty officer order 'Abandon ship!', forcing pyjama-clad boys into the cutters merely to impress the people in charge.

The new Captain Superintendent was a naval officer, Commander Matthew Bradby MBE. Though the routine he ordained was less harsh and without the idiosyncrasies that had characterised the Fry era – bare feet and cropped heads were things of the past – the expectations remained the same: hard work and disciplined effort. The curriculum was widened, and schoolmasters were employed whose duties were confined to the classroom. Under the old regime they had had to wear uniform, and had been expected to supervise boys in a wide range of activities; now there were specialist teachers of literature, science, history, geography, languages – all the normal subjects of good secondary schooling – who wore their own clothes and were not expected to double up as parade-ground disciplinarians.

Bradby was succeeded by Commander R. F. Hoyle in 1960, by which time the *Mercury* was in effect a residential grammar school, organised very much on the lines of a minor public school. The nautical ingredient in the curriculum was reduced to 25 per cent, and the end product was a young man who could think and perform over a wide range of subjects, and whose expectations were widened proportionately.

In 1968 the school was closed. By now it was the era of the large comprehensives, when a school as small as the place on the Hamble was deemed to be wildly uneconomic and out of date. Admiral of the Fleet the Earl Mountbatten of Burma, President of the ship in its final years, presided over the closing ceremonies. The boys were dispersed, mostly to the remaining grammar schools and to nautical colleges in other parts of the country.

Over the next few years the site was cleared to make way for Wimpey houses. Nothing was saved. The clock tower, for which

Beatie had dug the foundations, was bull-dozed into the ground. The little chapel which Charles Hoare had built had been destroyed by fire in 1952 and a new one had been built to replace it; but even this was swept away. The destruction of the theatre, of Beatie's Building, was undoubtedly a prime piece of architectural vandalism. The *Mercury* theatre was an architectural gem. It had unmistakably Teutonic lines, which would have looked good in a clearing in a Bavarian forest, but were so beautifully achieved that they were far from incongruous in an English setting. Inside, it was a place of simple elegance, from the white balustrade which separated orchestra from auditorium, to the curve of the balcony, worthy of the best theatres in the land. Schultz-Curtis, a German concert agent, loved this theatre, and used to say that for sheer beauty of sound and acoustical purity he would sooner bring his artists there than to any paradoxically, retreated into it as somewhere where they could be was in full command, it had been a haven for the boys who, paradoxically, retreated there as somewhere where they could be safe from the tyranny of the woman whose ideas and drive had brought it into being.

It was thus a hallowed place, having had added to design and utility an intrinsic worth that would not feature in an estate agent's accounts. The dancing, the plays, and, most of all, the great music that had been performed within its mellow walls had given it that precious intangible, a soul. To destroy the quiet glory, the simple splendour, of the temple which housed that soul must remain for those who loved it a piece of cold and unforgivable barbarism.

The dormitory ship on the river, the former HMS *Gannet*, later named *President*, was towed away in February 1970, and now lies at anchor in Gosport awaiting restoration as an 'up screw, down funnel' frigate of the 1870s, the only vessel of its type in existence.

The only other relics of the *Mercury* are the ship models collected by Charles Hoare and displayed in the National Maritime Museum, such as the royal yacht of 1685 in the Queen's House, and HMS

Tartar, twenty guns, built in 1734, a tiny craft in its glass case in Gallery Four, with every detail lovingly displayed by its maker, from the eponymous figure gripping the stem between his bare knees to the elaborate seven-windowed, carved stern.

If little of the physical *Mercury* remains, the spirit of the place is alive in the people who lived, taught and were taught there, or whose works endure even after their deaths. A deep impression has been made on the world of music by Eric McGavin, who left the ship shortly after the Second World War to join Boosey and Hawkes, the music publishers and makers of musical instruments. A brilliant clarinettist, he travelled the country lecturing on the clarinet and fostering the growth of music in schools that has led to the great youth orchestras of today. He himself founded the British Youth Wind Orchestra. He was made an honorary member of the Royal Academy of Music in recognition of his unique contribution to music in education. He died in 1970.

Of the thousands of men who began their careers on the *Mercury* many hold high positions in the Royal Navy, the Royal Marines and the Merchant Navy, and will for many years to come. Many are thriving in civilian life ashore. The youngest are in their early thirties, the oldest in their late eighties or early nineties. A growing number of them meet as members of an association dedicated to the restoration of their dormitory ship and to maintaining the friendships of their youth. They break down into two distinct groups: those of the Fry era, and those of the post-Fry era, with differing tales to tell of their youthful experiences. The older men, perhaps, try to awe the younger with stories of the incredible hardships endured under Mrs Fry, but all of them are bound by the common experience of having spent formative years in an establishment which had its origins in the struggle for freedom of a remarkable woman.

Katherine Whitehorn once wrote that 'freedom is messy', and in three words said more on the subject than a score of philosophers. It was the central paradox of the marriage of C. B. Fry and Beatie

Sumner that they both found a measure of freedom in it – one to amuse himself and, happily, a lot of others for most of his remaining years, the other to take up a work of worth in an area which, without that marriage, was closed to her. It was the central irony that the partner whose free choice was a life of duty and discipline, the very things her husband extolled as long as they did not include himself, may have ended up the freer and, perhaps, the more complete person.

In one of the few papers to survive her daughter's bonfire, Beatrice Holme Fry wrote three sentences which open a window, if ever so fractionally, on her character:

Notions and scruples are like spilt needles, making one afraid of treading, or sitting down, or even eating.

People glorify all sorts of bravery, except the bravery they might show on behalf of their nearest.

Failure after long perseverance is much grander than never to have a striving good enough to be called a failure.[4]

Perhaps together they constitute an acceptable epitaph.

Acknowledgements

A work of this nature involves many people – rather than books and journals – whose contributions one is bound and happy to acknowledge.

I am grateful to Mrs Jean Cook, Mr M. Hoare, Miss K. Potter and the committee of the *Mercury* Old Boys' Association for access to the collections of papers and pictures listed in my bibliography.

I spent a memorable afternoon with Stephen Fry, son of the late C. B. Fry. Sadly he died a few months after we met, but I trust his widow, Mrs Yvonne Fry, will accept my thanks for making our meeting possible. Joan Begbie and Mrs Adria Hoare, daughter-in-law of Charles Hoare, were ladies of great age when I met them in 1980 and have since died. Both contributed enormously to my research.

Dick Robinson grew up in the shadow of the *Mercury*. He helped me with information and with advice, as also did Mr and Mrs Tremlett of Kenn in Devon, whose home was once that of Margaret Baring Short, who married Charles Hoare in 1867.

The archivists, librarians and historians who helped are Sir Robin Mackworth-Young KCVO, FSA, Assistant Keeper of the Queen's Archives, Windsor, Mr D. J. H. Smith of Gloucester Public Record Office, Ashley Augier, the administrator of Stourhead House, John Munday of the National Maritime Museum, Mr C. R. Hiatt BA, ALA, Gloucester Library, Mr J. R. Wood FLA, AMBIM, Cheltenham Library, Dr Steven Blake, Cheltenham Museum, Stephen Green, the curator at Lords, the historian the Hon. Mrs S. Cubitt OBE, Mr Winder and Mr Lloyd of Hoare's Bank, Sue Heaster, Nottingham University Library, Mrs H. A. Scammell of the Isle of Wight Library, Dudley Jackson, Father Hockey, the writer and historian of Quarr Abbey, Mr D. M. Laverick FLA, Bromley Library, Mr G. Langley BA, FLA, Bristol Central Library, Mr F. I. Whyler, Bromley Historical Society, John Duthie of Aberdeen Art Gallery and Museum, Miss G. Beck, Mrs A. Doughty and Mr B. G. Thomas, all of the County Archives, Guildford, Dr T. R. Thompson FSA, FRHist SOC, Cricklade Historical Society, Major R. P. Rising RM, Royal Yacht Squadron, Dr Oswald Georg Bauer of the Bayreuthe Festspiele, and Sue Gregory of Trent Polytechnic Library.

Specialists in their respective fields who guided me are Lord Bathurst, Major-General D. H. G. Rice CBE of the Central Chancery of the Orders of Knighthood, Brigadier P. D. Fabin, Joint Honorary Secretary of the V.W.H., Mr J. Allen-Stevens MA, Mr K. Dyson, Manager of Nottingham Co-operative Bank, Mr J. C. Daukes, Clerk to the Governing Body, Charterhouse School, Mr J. Moore and Mr S. Cox, Dr Margaret Ezell, K. R. Arkell and J. Moore, the naval historians, the Revd Ben Hopkinson, Margaret Mann, Mr R. Lindley-Jones and Commander B. Bezance.

I exchanged letters with people on small but important points concerning the history of the *Mercury*. I treasure particularly a brief letter from the late Admiral of the Fleet the Earl Mountbatten of Burma. Similar aid came from Sr George Schuster, Mr C. S. L. Davis of Wadham College, Oxford, Mr A. E. L. Hill, the Rt Revd A. L. E. Hoskyns-Abrahall, and Mr F. W. Penny, formerly an instructor on the ship. I interviewed Mr Mills, also an instructor, just before his death in 1976. Others with whom I exchanged letters are: Mr R. S. Wilson, Mr J. R. Goudge, Captain G. Sutton, Mr I. Dodd, Canon Woodhall, Mr A. L. Morris, Andrew McGavin, Cecil Fawcett, George Prince, Mr B. W. Ames, Madeline Attwood, Mrs M. Briggs, Mr A. W. Chaplin, Captain A. H. Cooke, David Cook, Mr H. W. Cookson, Mr W. Downing, George Hoare, Vera Fisher, Josephine Gibbs, the Revd R. L. Hendry, Brenda Hoare, Mrs Hooker, Mr A. F. Jaques, Phyllis Keyte, Mr R. C. Payne, Mr and Mrs N. Robinson, Mr B. Stocken, Zena Thomas, Mabel Whitcombe, Mr R. J. Williams, Mr R. S. Wren, Lieutenant-Commander P. Whitlock, and Mr P. Dimmick, who taught at the *Mercury* in its closing years.

I must make particular mention of the men whose letters covered events at the *Mercury* before, during and after the First World War. They are Mr L. G. Charles, Mr L. A. West, Commander A. H. Horrell RN, Mr R. Sinfield, Captain R. E. Hutchins CBE, DSC, RN, Lieutenant W. Mobsby RN, Mr E. R. Hunter and Mr E. Walker. To all the above I express my heartfelt thanks.

The staff of Girton College, Cambridge, were my hosts during a sabbatical at the university in 1978 when I began the major research for my book. I take this opportunity to record my thanks for their hospitality during that period.

I am grateful to Eyre and Spottiswoode Ltd for giving me permission to quote from *Life Worth Living* by C. B. Fry and from *F. E.: The Life of F. E. Smith, First Earl of Birkenhead* by Lord Birkenhead; to William Collins Ltd for permission to quote from *Autobiography* by Neville Cardus and *Sort of a Cricketing Person* by E. W. Swanton; to William Heinemann Ltd for permission to quote from *The English* by J. B. Priestley; to Weidenfeld & Nicolson Ltd for permission to quote from *Memories* by Maurice Bowra; and to Constable Ltd for permission to quote from *A History of the VWH Country* by Earl Bathurst.

My final acknowledgement must record the special support given to me by Jean Cook, Colin Ridge, and Dr Val Benton. Jean and Colin invited me to their homes to stay for days at a time during the long period when I was in London and the south looking for material. Colin has since died, and I send my lasting thanks to his widow, Beatrice, for sharing with me the company of a marvellous man. Val Benton, recently retired as Head of English at Trent Polytechnic College, supported and advised me in the major revisions of the text which brought it finally to the notice of a publisher. I remain forever in her debt.

Ronald Morris
Cambridge University 1978
Chilwell 1984

Bibliography and references

Batchelor, Denzil, *C. B. Fry* (in the series 'Cricketing Lives'), London, 1951.
Bathurst, the seventh Earl, *A History of the V.W.H. Country*, London, 1936.
Birkenhead, the second Earl, *F.E., The Life of F. E. Smith, First Earl of Birkenhead*, London, 1959.
Bowra, Sir Maurice, *Memories*, London, 1966.
Cardus, Sir Neville, *Autobiography*, London, 1961.
Fry, C. B., *Life Worth Living*, London, 1939.
Gardner, Henry, Unpublished MS, *autobiography*, in the National Maritime Museum.
McGavin Papers, Unpublished collection, property of Mrs Jean Cook.
Margaret Hoare Collection, Unpublished collection of newspaper cuttings, property of Michael Hoare.
Mercury Old Boys' Association Papers, Unpublished collection of papers, property of M.O.B.A.
Kingscote Papers, Unpublished collection of papers, property of Miss K. Potter.
Priestley, J. B., *The English*, London, 1973.
Swanton, E. W., *Sort of a Cricketing Person*, London, 1972.

REFERENCES

MHNC: Margaret Hoare Newspaper Collection

Chapter 1
1 – John Arlott, in *Hampshire Magazine*, August 1971, p. 27.
2 – J. B. Priestley, *The English*, p. 236.
3 – McGavin papers.

Chapter 2
1 – Denzil Batchelor, *C. B. Fry*, p. 8.
2 – MHNC.

3 – *Hants Independent*, 23 May 1908.
4 – MHNC.

Chapter 3
1 – Bathurst, *A History of the V.W.H. Country*, p. 152.
2 – ibid., p. 153.
3 – MHNC.
4 – ibid.
5 – ibid.
6 – ibid.
7 – ibid.
8 – Potter collection of letters.
9 – MHNC.
10 – ibid.
11 – ibid.
12 – ibid.
13 – *Gloucester Chronicle*, 21 March 1885.
14 – Charles Scott. Affidavit in P.R.O., J.4/2685/1486, 1881.
15 – Beatrice Holme Sumner. Affidavit in P.R.O., J4/2685/1419, 1885.
16 – ibid.
17 – ibid.
18 – Fitzhardinge Kingscote. Affidavit in P.R.O., J4/2416/2984 001428, 1884.
19 – James Kennelly. Affidavit in P.R.O., J4/2416/2983.
20 – Fitzhardinge Kingscote. Affidavit in P.R.O., 1884.
21 – Beatrice Holme Sumner. Affidavit in P.R.O., 1885.
22 – Alfred Inderwick. Affidavit in P.R.O., J4/2686/1575, 1885.
23 – Fitzhardinge Kingscote. Affidavit in P.R.O., 1884.

Chapter 4
1 – MHNC.
2 – Alfred Inderwick. Affidavit in P.R.O., 1885.
3 – Charles Hoare. Affidavit in P.R.O., J4/2419/3728, 1884.
4 – Bathurst, op. cit., p. 164.
5 – ibid., p. 162.
6 – ibid., p. 160.
7 – *Hants Independent*, 23 May 1908.
8 – Bathurst, op. cit., p. 162.
9 – MHNC.

10 – Bathurst papers, Gloucester Record Office, Box E, No. 163.
11 – Bathurst, op. cit., p. 165.
12 – Fitzhardinge Kingscote. Affidavit in P.R.O., 1884.
13 – James Kennelly. Affidavit, 1884.
14 – Robert Blott. Affidavit in P.R.O., J4/2685/1494, 1884.
15 – Hoare, Affidavit, 1884.
16 – *Wilts and Gloucestershire Standard*, 16 August 1884.
17 – ibid.
18 – Law Reports, 17 March 1885.

Chapter 5

1 – *The Times*, 18 March 1885.
2 – Beatrice Holme Sumner. Affidavit, 1885.
3 – ibid.
4 – Rt Hon. The Marchioness of Cholmondeley. Affidavit in P.R.O., J4/
    2686/1503, 1885.
5 – Alfred Inderwick. Affidavit in P.R.O., J4/2416/2990.
6 – Nigel Kingscote. Affidavit in P.R.O., J4/2416/2990, 1885.
7 – A. R. Huitt. Affidavit in P.R.O., J4/2685/1420, 1885.
8 – For accounts of the case, see *The Times*, 18 and 19 March 1885;
    Gloucestershire Chronicle, 21 March 1885; *The People*, 22 March 1885;
    Reynolds Newspaper, 22 March 1885; *News of the World*, 22 March 1885.
9 – Sumner *v*. Kingscote (1885) 1 T.L.R. 351.
10 – *Truth*, 26 March 1885.
11 – *Vanity Fair*, 21 March 1885, p. 167.

Chapter 6

1 – *Wilts and Gloucestershire Standard*, 2 May 1885.
2 – J. Moore of Bulmer, Yorkshire, in letters to the author.
3 – MHNC.
4 – Bathurst papers.
5 – Bathurst, op. cit., p. 182.
6 – ibid., p. 183.
7 – ibid., p. 183.

Chapter 7

1 – *Mercury* Old Boys' Association (MOBA) collection of papers ('Voyage to
    Villefranche' etc.).

2 – Lord Rosebery, quoted in J. B. Priestley, op. cit., p. 72.
3 – McGavin papers, undated programme (*c.* 1927).
4 – McGavin papers. Quoted in *Mercury* theatre programme, November 1927; original written 20 July 1897.
5 – Plaque preserved at Rhinefield House, Hants.

Chapter 8
1 – Birkenhead, *F.E.*, *The Life of F. E. Smith, First Earl of Birkenhead*, p. 31.
2 – ibid., p. 30.
3 – C. B. Fry, *Life Worth Living*, pp. 76–7.
4 – Sir George Schuster, in a letter to the author.
5 – MOBA papers.
6 – Fry, op. cit., p. 53.
7 – ibid., p. 280.
8 – L. G. Charles, in letter to the author.
9 – *Southern Daily Echo*, 8 September 1956.
10 – *Mercury Magazine*, 1907–8.
11 – ibid.

Chapter 9
1 – A. R. Cooper, in *The Captain* (editor C. B. Fry), May 1909.
2 – Lytton Strachey, *Eminent Victorians*, 1918.
3 – Fry, op. cit., pp. 190–1.
4 – Adria Hoare: from an interview with the author.
5 – Fry, op. cit., pp. 188–90.
6 – J. Moore: original research on behalf of the author.
7 – MOBA Collection.

Chapter 10
1 – E. Walker, in letters to the author.
2 – MOBA Collection.
3 – Henry Gardner, *Autobiography*, 1979.
4 – C. Ridge, in letters to the author.
5 – Fry, op. cit., p. 195.
6 – E. P. Hunter, in letters to the author.
7 – *Mercury Magazine*, December 1926.
8 – ibid.

9 – ibid.
10 – *Mercury Magazine*, December 1928.
11 – *Mercury Magazine*, 1931.
12 – ibid.
13 – ibid.
14 – ibid.
15 – ibid.
16 – *Mercury Magazine*, December 1921.
17 – *Mercury Magazine*, October 1926.
18 – Captain R. E. Hutchins, RN, in letters to the author.

Chapter 11
1 – Royal Archives, Windsor.
2 – Admiral of the Fleet the Rt Hon. the Earl Mountbatten of Burma, in a letter to the author.
3 – National Maritime Museum: a collection of letters about the Hoare Collection of ship models.
4 – E. Walker, in letters to the author.
5 – Lieutenant W. Mobsby, RN, in letters to the author.
6 – E. W. Swanton, *Sort of a Cricketing Person*, p. 188.
7 – Stephen Fry, in an interview with the author.
8 – National Maritime Museum, newspaper archives, 23 February 1934.
9 – Neville Cardus, *Autobiography*, p. 150.
10 – Fry, op. cit., p. 369.
11 – ibid., p. 369.
12 – ibid., p. 377.
13 – ibid., p. 193.
14 – ibid., p. 179.

Chapter 12
1 – Captain Ronald A. Hopwood RN, *The Laws of the Navy*.
2 – McGavin papers.
3 – *Southern Daily Echo*, 23 April 1946.
4 – McGavin papers.
5 – *Mercury Magazine*, 1927.
6 – McGavin papers.
7 – ibid.

Epilogue
1 – Samuel Johnson, *Lives of the Poets*.
2 – Maurice Bowra, *Memories*, p. 143.
3 – Birkenhead, op. cit., p. 32.
4 – McGavin papers.

Index